wide awake

ERWIN McMANUS

Thomas Nelson
Since 1798

NASHVILLE   DALLAS   MEXICO CITY   RIO DE JANEIRO   BEIJING

Wide Awake

© 2008 by Erwin Raphael McManus

Published in Nashville, Tennessee, by Thomas Nelson. Thomas Nelson is a registered trademark of Thomas Nelson, Inc.

Published in association with Yates & Yates, www.yates2.com.

Artwork throughout the book is used by permission of Dany Paragouteva, www.danydesign.net

Author photo © Jess Barnard. Used by permission.

Thomas Nelson, Inc., titles may be purchased in bulk for educational, business, fund-raising, or sales promotional use. For information, please e-mail SpecialMarkets@ThomasNelson.com.

Unless otherwise marked, Scripture quotations are taken from The Holy Bible, New Living Translation, © 1996. Used by permission of Tyndale House Publishers, Inc., Wheaton, IL 60189. All rights reserved.

Scripture quotations marked NIV are taken from the HOLY BIBLE: NEW INTERNATIONAL VERSION®. © 1973, 1978, 1984 by International Bible Society. Used by permission of Zondervan Publishing House. All rights reserved.

Scripture quotations marked TNIV are taken from the HOLY BIBLE, TODAY'S NEW INTERNATIONAL VERSION®. © 2001, 2005 by International Bible Society. Used by permission of Zondervan. All rights reserved.

Scripture quotations marked NASB are taken from NEW AMERICAN STANDARD BIBLE®, © The Lockman Foundation 1960, 1962, 1963, 1968, 1971, 1972, 1973, 1975, 1977, 1995. Used by permission.

ISBN 978-1-4002-8036-0 (IE)

Library of Congress Cataloging-in-Publication Data

McManus, Erwin Raphael.
 Wide awake : the future is waiting within you / Erwin Raphael McManus.
  p. cm.
 ISBN 978-0-7852-1495-3
 1. Dreams—Religious aspects—Christianity. 2. Vocation—Christianity. I. Title.
BR115.D74M36 2008
248.4—dc22   2008009195

Printed in the United States of America

08 09 10 11 12 RRD 5 4 3 2 1

To my fellow sojourner,

David Arcos

For two decades we have journeyed together.

On this quest to create

we have dreamed and lived

facing great challenges.

We have shared failure and success

sorrow and joy

tears and laughter.

You are both hero and human

the best of both.

You are the consummate proof that it is possible to live wide awake.

Keep dreaming with your eyes open.

To my great friend.

Your brother,

Erwin

contents

acknowledgments

THANKS TO ALL THE CREW AT MOSAIC WHO REPRESENT the community from which so much of the lessons learned and stories lived have come. Also the team of friends that make up Awaken have been invaluable to all of us who love to dream and see those dreams become reality.

Individuals who have really made this book and the companion film project come together are: Holly Quillen, Alisah Duran, Jason Jaggard, Dany Paragouteva, Joby Harris, Jess Barnard, Ruthi Auda, Tammy Borrero, Keith Cox, Jimmy and Samantha Duke, Chris Thomason, Jeana Ledbetter, and, of course, my family—my wife Kim and my son and daughter Aaron and Mariah.

Also my thanks to Yates & Yates, Thomas Nelson Publishers, Indelible Media group, and Lionsgate.

And to those who live *wide awake,* I would encourage you to search out:

Glare of Rockets, myspace.com/glareofrockets

City of Others, city-of-others.com

To Write Love on Her Arms, twloha.com

Until June, untiljune.com

Mosaic Podcasts, mosaic.org/podcast

She Strength / She Community, shecommunity.org

The Origins Project, theoriginsproject.org

The Crave film series, soulcravings.com

Wide Awake Records, wideawakerecords.com

Chris Duran, chrisduranmusic.com

Eric Michael Bryant, ericbryant.org

TOMS Shoes, tomsshoes.com

awaken

THE HERO

DAVID. *(to Elijah)* This morning was the first morning I can remember, that I didn't open my eyes and feel that sadness. . . . I thought the person who wrote that note had an answer for me.

ELIJAH. *(to David)* That little bit of sadness in the mornings you spoke of? I think I know what that is. Perhaps you're not doing what you're supposed to be doing.

—— M. Night Shyamalan's film *Unbreakable*

Unbreakable is a fictional story about a seemingly ordinary person who discovers he is nothing less than a superhero. This clever film is wrapped around the premise that graphic novels—comic books—are based on the exploits of individuals who live and work among us. It has been years since I saw this film, yet these lines have remained with me. They resonated far more deeply than I care to admit.

For years, I woke each day with a sadness I couldn't shake, and then more sadness met me the moment I crawled out of bed. Thankfully, it is not so today. My best dreams are no longer wasted on my sleep. I find myself closing my eyes each night, eagerly waiting for tomorrow to come. There is nothing like feeling fully alive and dreaming wide awake. I am living a life beyond my wildest dreams—and I had some wild dreams.

Yet every day, I meet people who appear happy and are by every perceivable measure successful—but in the mornings, just before they face the world, they are greeted by that little bit of sadness. Los Angeles, my home, is filled with stark reminders that even for the most talented and ambitious, fulfillment can be elusive if not impossible to find. It is here, where Marilyn Monroe and James Dean serve as our icons, that we find the boulevard of broken dreams.

Many of us struggle to find a dream that doesn't turn out to be a nightmare. Or we find ourselves shipwrecked when our dreams come true, but they were nothing like what we thought. We were sure this was the life we always wanted—the life we would kill for. Instead, it almost kills us.

For fifteen years, I have served as the spiritual and life mentor for our community of faith known as Mosaic. Thousands of deeply sincere, passionate, talented, bright, and immensely gifted people journey with us in pursuing the life God has created us to live. They are people with great dreams and the courage to back them up. But the process of finding the right dream and then moving it into life sometimes keeps them from making their dreams a reality. With an average age of twenty-five, our community is 90 percent energy and 10 percent experience. These are the cream of the crop, and sharing life together has reinforced the need for *Wide Awake*—because even the best of us can find turning our dreams into reality elusive and even overwhelming.

For a long time I have felt the weight of calling people to pursue their dreams, to take great risks, and to live a life beyond their imagination. But the devil, of course, is in the details—or in this case, in the process. Many people have told me they are now in hot pursuit of dreams long forgotten, but just as many ask me to please explain how exactly they can make their dreams a reality.

There are too many amazing people with unfilled lives and unfulfilled dreams. It's as if I keep meeting M. Night's David, who has yet to discover he is more than he knows. I may not know you personally, but this I know about you without question—there is a hero within you waiting to be awakened.

Awaken Humanity

Over the years, we at Awaken have been privileged to invest in hundreds of thousands, if not millions, of people around the world. We are able to see quickly the extraordinary potential of those we come in contact with. I have come to the place where I simply think of every human being as pre-great. Whether in poverty or wealth, whether educated formally or informally, whether from the Americas or Africa or Australia, I have found the same result—people are the most underused and undervalued resource on this planet.

Earth's unlimited resource is the gifts, talent, passions, imagination, and ingenuity of its citizens. You would think we would know this by now, but we often seem to miss the gift right in front of us. The world needs you to find the hero within you. The real battle is not between good and evil but between less and more. Most of us don't choose the worst life; we just don't choose the best. We can't afford for you to sleep through your dreams. It is my hope that this book can help you find your way to a life worth living.

But let me be honest with you: my motivation is much broader, much bigger than this. The world needs you at your best. This planet is made better or worse by the people we choose to become. If you live a diminished life, it's not only you who loses, but the world loses, and humanity loses. There is a story to be written by your life, and though it may never inspire a graphic novel, it is a heroic tale nonetheless. Though you may not recognize it, there is greatness within you.

In the pages to come, we will begin a pilgrimage in search of that hero within you waiting to be awakened. Specifically, we will explore eight attributes that are necessary to live out your greatness. I can help you discover them, but only you can choose to rise up and embrace your destiny. Very few are meant for a life of notoriety, yet all of us are meant for a life of significance. We should never confuse fame with greatness. The former is about what you do for yourself; the latter is about what you do for others. It is in this way that all of us have heroic lives to live. We are all called to serve the greater good.

I am convinced if you begin to live wide awake, you will no longer be haunted by that little bit of sadness in the mornings. In its place will be a sense of awe that your life could be so extraordinary. Your life may not be any easier, and you may not be wealthier or finally have that house in Malibu. But you will know that you must get out of bed and live wide awake every day, because there is so much to be done.

When we live wide awake, the world begins to reflect the kind of place in which God intended us to live. After all, he placed us in paradise and expected us to take care of his creation—so much for a good start. Now we need to step up and reclaim what was lost. Jesus came to bring out the best in us. When this happens, we should expect that everything else will change for the better.

We need to live wide awake because there are diseases killing millions and we need to find a cure, famines leaving multitudes starving and we need to provide food, economies leaving families homeless and we need to create opportunities for work and wealth, genocide that must be stopped, slavery that must be ended, water wells that must be dug, children who need to be loved, relationships that need to be healed, elderly who need to be cared for, beauty that needs to be created, futures that need to be saved, and dreams that we must not let die or go unfulfilled.

There is a future that needs to be created, and it is waiting for you and me to wake up and get out of bed. The alarm has sounded, and it is time to shake off the slumber.

You know that little bit of sadness that greets you in the mornings? Maybe it's there because you're not doing what you're supposed to be doing. You're not living the life you're supposed to be living. You're not dreaming wide awake. It's your soul searching for its hero.

dream 1

THE ARTIST

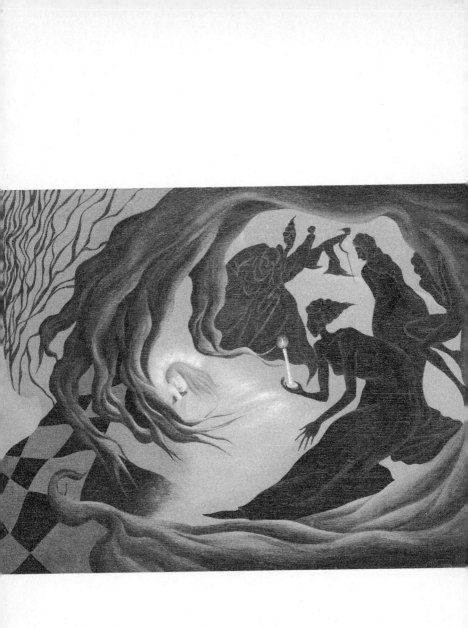

IT FELT LIKE MY OWN MOUNT OF TRANSFIGURATION. I was sharing a meal with Moses, Noah, and Philemon, eating in majestic surroundings outside of Arusha, Tanzania. We were the world sitting at the table—one from Ethiopia, one from Nigeria, one from Tanzania, and myself from El Salvador.

A community of global entrepreneurs had gathered to listen and learn and talk and dream about the future of Africa. Moses, I learned, was a world-renowned scientist. Philemon was a film-maker, and Noah a technology pioneer. All of us had one thing in common: we are all dreamers. I will never forget the amazing two hours I spent with these men. Especially Noah. He was the most gracious and natural host of the table—eager to care for everyone and make us feel that we belonged. I can't imagine anyone feeling as if he was not Noah's lifelong friend and ally.

After a while, I asked Noah what he did for a living. He asked me if I had ever heard of XM Radio, and I said of course. He casually explained that was his venture.

"So you head up XM?"

"No, I got out right after. That's not what I'm interested in."

He had my full attention. "So what are you doing now?"

"I'm the founder of WorldSpace, the parent company that started XM Radio."

He went on to explain that he saw his people—the people of Africa—dying needlessly. They were dying due to ignorance, due to lack of information. He wanted to do something about it. He talked to his wife, and she agreed. "So I left my job, my security, everything."

He did all this to pursue a dream that was born out of a burden.

"We had nothing but an idea that had never been done. Starting with nothing, we raised one and a half billion dollars in eighteen months."

I was struck by one of the world's most cutting-edge technologies starting not in Japan or the United States or in a highly developed country, but out of Africa. For us, radio is nothing more than entertainment—for Noah, it's life.

I will never forget Ethiopian-born Noah Samara.

A dreamer.

A dreamer who dreams of a better world.

A dreamer who dreams of a better world and risks everything to make it happen.

To create a different world is both a courageous act and a creative act. Life is a work of art. The canvas you paint first is your life. Then your life becomes the brush from which you paint that part of the world you touch while you are here on this planet. You are an artist. What work of art will you leave behind?

Some spend their lives painting images that only remember the past. Their dreams are a memorial to what was. Others live in regret and dream only of what could have been. Their art is a tribute to a world that we can only envy.

Still there are those who dream of a world that does not yet exist; of a world that must exist. They dream a future that must be created. They are the artists of which this chapter speaks. The ones who dream wide awake.

If your dreams became the future of humanity, would this be a better world?

Imagine this:
> the future of humanity
>> could be an idea
>>> in someone's mind
>>>> right now.

Maybe that's one reason Jesus tells us to come to him like little children.

> They have the best
>> imaginations.

Remember your dreams? What would the world look like if our best dreams became the world we lived in? I am far too much of a realist to believe all our dreams can come true. But is it possible we have underestimated the power of dreams? Science is discovering the extraordinary capacity of the human brain, and Scripture clearly points to the mind as the context for all change. The opening verses of Romans 12 remind us that our transformation is directly connected to the renewing of our minds. It's curious that while our imagination is not limited, our thinking so often is.

Whatever else we need to do to live the life of our dreams, I know this: we can't just lie there. You can't just sit back and hope that the life you long for will simply come to you. To live wide awake you have to begin with a dream; but it doesn't end there.

We're not talking about sleepwalking. We're talking about dreaming with our eyes open.

DREAMS OF FLYING

I remember the day like it was yesterday—in fact, I remember the exact day: February 23, 1977. It was the day after my car broke down, and my aunt volunteered to drive me to work. She decided not to get off on the exit ramp. Instead, she pulled over on the side of the road and asked if I could get out there. No problem. This way she could keep going, and I could just hop over to work. When I jumped out of her VW bug, I saw a UPS truck coming down the highway and quickly assessed that I could outrun the slow, brown truck. I'm not the most patient person in the world, so I just took off running across the freeway.

I was speedier than the UPS truck, but I didn't see the car that was accelerating to pass from the left. I think it was a Monte Carlo—I never actually saw it. But I did hear it. I heard brakes (well, technically I heard the sound of burning rubber grabbing concrete) screeching to a halt, and somehow I knew those brakes were screaming at me. I jumped as high as I could, hoping to clear the vehicle, hoping it wasn't another truck. I cleared the hood of the car. Later I was informed that if I had not jumped, I would have been killed instantly. Jumping kept me from being crushed, and I instead hit the windshield. Or that's what they tell me, at least.

I can't imagine what the driver was thinking. All of a sudden, he sees this human being soaring toward him in the air. I hit the windshield and went flying across a couple of lanes (or as Buzz Lightyear would describe it, falling with style). I had always dreamed of flying, but this wasn't exactly what I had in mind. I started thinking about how when I was a long jumper, we experimented with doing flips in the air to increase our distance. So as I hit the air, I balled up and tried to roll forward when I landed on the concrete. I finally came to a halt and just lay there in the middle of the street. I heard cars everywhere and realized I was blocking oncoming traffic.

My poor aunt, in her VW bug, saw all this happen. I imagine she was thinking that her sister, my mom, was going to kill her for losing her son. So she made a U-turn right in the middle of the highway, got out of the car, ran over to me, and yelled, "Get up, and I'll take you to the hospital!" I was lying there, thinking, *If I could get up, I wouldn't have to go to the hospital.*

I could see she was panicking. She looked like the one who was in shock. I desperately wanted to pass out and surrender to unconsciousness, but her distress kept me conscious. I felt I somehow needed to help her through this. I said, "I can't get up."

Quickly after—I don't know how much time actually went by—two ambulances arrived: one was a county ambulance, and the other was a city ambulance. I was sort of in a daze, but I remember the paramedics arguing about which district I was in. It seemed I happened to be lying on the city/county line. I was lying on the ground, and I could hear them arguing with each other. I guess they worked on commission.

Finally, they asked me, "Which hospital do you want to go to?"

I said, "Well, which one's cheaper?" I was eighteen years old, paying my own bills, trying to make it through life. I was thinking, *This is going to cost me a lot of money.* I should have said, "Which one is better?" but that's not what came to mind.

They said, "County."

I said, "Take me to county."

They brought over the little gurney and laid me on top, put me in the ambulance, and drove me to the hospital. I was paralyzed from the waist down; I had no feeling anywhere from the belt down. So they put me in the emergency room, ran all the tests, stuck my foot with the prickly thing, and slapped me around. I felt nothing. No pain, no feeling, nothing. Two limbs just lying there. It was a little scary to be a teenager and wondering if I would ever walk again.

Some time passed, and my mom and my stepdad came. The doctors explained, "We have to take some tests and do X-rays and see if there's some kind of spinal damage."

Then it happened. I had to go to the bathroom. And if anyone knows me, I am sort of a private person; I don't like going to the bathroom in front of people.

So I asked, "Could you guys put me in a wheelchair and take me to the bathroom?"

They said, "No, we can't move you."

I said, "Look, I have to go to the bathroom."

They brought me this little kidney-shaped thing and said, "Well, you have to go in this."

I said, "I'm not going to the bathroom in that."

"Yes, you are," they insisted.

I begged them, "Will you please help me get to the toilet? This is desperate!"

They said, "We can't move you. You have to stay in this bed."

So I conceded. As a compromise, I asked, "Will you guys at least give me some privacy?"

So they closed the curtain and waited outside, but that sheet is not soundproof. I was not going to relieve myself with everybody and his brother standing on the other side of the curtain. So I insisted they leave the area completely. Everyone had to leave for this to work—nurse, parents, everyone. They all finally accommodated my demand for privacy and dignity and left the semi-private room that served as their ER.

"Close the door," I half-yelled. It clicked shut. I was lying there with this little kidney-shaped toilet and thinking, *I am not going to the bathroom in this thing.*

Have you ever seen an emergency room bed? Those things are high. I mean really high! I am stranded there on that bed, and I cannot move anything from the waist down. I am desperate and determined to get to the bathroom. I started swinging myself side to side on the bed, trying to get some momentum. Finally I was able to roll myself off the bed, and I hit that hard, cold hospital floor without anything to cushion my fall. At least it didn't hurt from the waist down.

I lay there, caught my breath, and started crawling across the emergency room with my hands. Then I began slithering down by the other beds, looking back and hoping no one would see me. Working my way the opposite direction from where they waited I finally made it down the emergency room, turned left, and saw a bathroom right there. It was one of those moments when I knew there was a God—and he was merciful. I worked my way into the bathroom, dragging my legs behind me, and then closed the door.

I entered into a relationship with the commode I never had before.

I grabbed it and pulled myself up. I could only hope that someone had cleaned it right before. I finally got on that toilet and had a divine moment. Then it hit me: *I'm stuck here. I can't move.* I considered screaming for help, but that would be very humiliating. So I sat there for a while, and then I started pushing on the toilet, and then I stood up, and I walked out. It wasn't flying, but it would do for now.

I have never fully understood what happened that day except to realize that long before I was looking for God, he was looking out for me.

I've looked back and wondered many times, if I hadn't been so stubborn, so determined, so desperate to go to the bathroom on my own terms, how long would I have lain on that bed? Now, I'm not saying that everyone who is lying on a bed or sitting in a wheelchair could get up and walk, but I am saying this: sometimes the limitations you are willing to accept establish the boundaries of your existence.

The doctors couldn't see me getting out of that bed, and I couldn't see myself staying in that bed. You ever notice that sometimes your desire to accomplish something can pull you through? Ever notice that people who refuse to give up seem to succeed the most? Ever notice that people who expect great things seem most likely to accomplish great things? If your dreams are supposed to be bigger than your life, then your life will always be limited by the size of your dreams.

Sometimes getting up and walking is more about your head than your legs.

I don't understand everything that happened that day. I am certainly grateful to God for allowing me to walk out of that hospital, but I know part of it was that I simply would not allow my life to be defined by what others said I could not do. Hey, sometimes they're right—it can't be done. But that doesn't mean it shouldn't be attempted. There are times you have to see yourself and your future differently than everyone else. You have to be willing to dream of a life that seems unlikely or maybe even impossible.

What you expect from yourself and your life has a direct effect on what you will get out of life. How you imagine yourself and your future has a huge effect on what actually happens. Creating the life of your dreams begins with the dream. It begins with the ability to imagine yourself differently than you are and your life differently than it is.

DREAMS TO SLEEP ON

Somewhere in our past, many of us gave up on our dreams and lost touch with this essential part of our being. Sometimes our capacity to dream of a different us, of a different life, is beaten up and left broken by people and pain and disappointment. Sometimes what should be a dream inspiring us is actually a fantasy distracting us. Say, for instance, if you're waiting to be abducted by aliens from outer space and have been giving your whole life to this dream, it's probably safe to say this is not a life well spent.

Have you ever met someone who was pursuing the wrong dream? You know, it's the *American Idol* syndrome. You are so sure of your talent and are waiting to be discovered, but even your friends don't like to hear you sing. You might want to ask yourself, *Is this a dream or just a fantasy?*

It's one thing to want to be an Olympic sprinter when you're young, even when your aversion to sweat and pain should give you a clue that it may not be the right dream for your life; but you let the fantasy sort of roll along. Or say, if you're not at least pushing six feet, you probably shouldn't be aspiring to make it in the NBA (unless you're Muggsy Bogues or Earl Boykins). It may be more of a fantasy than a dream. Especially if you also can't dribble, pass, or shoot.

No matter what the dangers or downsides of dreaming, it is more devastating to the human spirit to give up on our dreams altogether. When your dreams are aligned with your talent, you are postured to not only dream big, but live big. So if you are 5'7 and the NBA is your dream and you have what it takes, don't let the odds dissuade you—go ahead and be defiant and prove us all wrong. The bigger people dream, the bigger they tend to live. And this is without adding God to the formula. When you begin to understand that you are at the core a spiritual being, it begins to make sense why you need the Source of all creativity active in your life to fully live out your God-given potential.

For centuries now, Jesus has been a focus of every kind of research, from theology to history to philosophy. His approach to ethics left an undeniable mark on humanity. What has been significantly underappreciated is how Jesus changed the way his followers actually engaged life. He launched a movement that
unleashed previously untapped
potential
in those who believed
in him.
He created an environment
where his disciples began
to believe the impossible
and soon found they were
turning dreams into
reality.
His became a movement of dreamers
and visionaries called and
compelled to dream
of a better world.

He called them to touch the whole of humanity with his message of life and love. Theirs was a life of faith and a call to accomplish great things by serving humanity. Here, by the way, is one of the dramatic differences between Jesus and Buddha. Buddha once wrote, "Do not dwell in the past, do not dream of the future, concentrate the mind on the present moment."

While I agree we must not dwell in the past, and I wrote an entire book on how to live and seize the power of every moment, I have to say, Buddha missed it when it comes to the future—not to mention the power of dreams. Our dreams are where the future is fueled and created. This is one of the things I love about Jesus and the Scriptures—they call us to dream and to dream with our eyes open. To live wide awake you have to begin to dream. You have to dare to dream great dreams and find the courage to live them.

WHAT DO YOU WANT?

In the gospel of Mark, we read two conversations that are seemingly disconnected but are actually the same. Both of them involve people who were asking Jesus for something.

The first conversation is between Jesus and two of his disciples, John and James. Jesus has just opened up his soul to these guys. He's told them he's going to Jerusalem; he's going to have to suffer; he's going to become the sacrifice for all of humanity; he's going to be crucified, killed, and raised from the dead. And his words seem to go right over the disciples' heads.

Right after that, John and James come to Jesus and say, "Lord, we want you to do for us whatever we ask." Did you ever do that to your parents when you were a kid? "I want you to make me a promise," you'd say, which is translated, "I want you to do something for me that you would not want to do if you knew before you promised."

"What do you want?" your parents would say.

"Promise first, and then I'll tell you. Say yes first."

I wonder how many of us have done this. We want someone to commit to us before we actually tell the person what we want. That's what John and James were doing. "Jesus, we want an upfront yes. Will you do for us what we want?"

Jesus asks them, "What do you want?" They answer, "When you are on your throne in your kingdom, we want to sit at your right hand and your left hand." In other words, *we want to be in charge.* Their thinking makes perfect sense. Jesus is a king. Every king eventually has a kingdom. Being king is a lot of work. Jesus is going to need good people to help him run things. John and James are early investors and want to stake their claim before the field gets too crowded. It's good, old-fashioned cronyism.

Jesus says to John and James, "You don't even know what you are asking. Can you really bear the suffering I'm going to bear?" They assure him, "Oh yes, Lord, we will. We can, yes." Of course they didn't know what they would be getting. They wanted power and prestige, but Jesus was offering servanthood and sacrifice.

Jesus tells John and James that those positions are not for him to give, but for his Father to decide. I think that was a nice way of saying, *Not on your life.*

There are dreams we try to recruit God into, and frankly I think he looks at us and says, *Not on your life.* God is not going to invest himself in a dream fueled by greed, arrogance, self-indulgence, and self-centeredness. Jesus spent much of his influence trying to get those who would listen to change what they cared about.

Because what you care about

is what you dream about.

Your passions fuel your dreams.

God doesn't say yes to everything we ask, because our dreams need to be fueled by the right things. Some dreams aren't worth losing sleep over. Still, there are dreams you had better not sleep through. When God is at the core of our lives, he becomes the inspirer of our dreams. If we want to live the wide awake life of our dreams, we must trust God to guide us on a journey we cannot take on our own.

Where are your dreams coming from? Who or what is informing your dreams? How do you discern between the dreams of your slumber and the dreams of your soul? To find this dream is to find your life. So unlike Freud, let's forget interpreting your dreams and begin a search for them.

After this story there's an interlude about a blind man who interrupts Jesus and his disciples. A great crowd was following Jesus, and a blind beggar named Bartimaeus ("son of Timaeus") was sitting beside the road as Jesus was passing by.

"When Bartimaeus heard that Jesus from Nazareth was nearby, he began to shout out, 'Jesus, Son of David, have mercy on me!' 'Be quiet!' some of the people yelled at him. But he only shouted louder, 'Son of David, have mercy on me!'"

When Jesus heard him, he stopped and called Bartimaeus to come to him. "So they called the blind man. 'Cheer up,' they said. 'Come on, he's calling you!' Bartimaeus threw aside his coat, jumped up, and came to Jesus."

Then Jesus asked him this question: "What do you want me to do for you?".

Now isn't that a strange question? I mean, a blind man walks up to him, and Jesus asks, "What do you want me to do for you?" To begin with, Jesus is supposed to be God. Shouldn't he already know what the blind man wants? But even if he wasn't God and he was just intuitive, surely, with a blind guy standing in front of Him, what Bartimaeus wants would be pretty obvious. It's not like he's going to say, "Lord, I would like to hear better to compensate for my blindness." Or, "Well, Lord, you know when I got up and I left my coat back there. Can I have a new coat?"

Jesus asks, "What do you want from me?"

I love the way it's written here: "'Teacher,' the blind man said, 'I want to see!' And Jesus said to him, 'Go your way. Your faith has healed you.' Instantly the blind man could see! Then he followed Jesus down the road."

Why make something so obvious a point of emphasis? It's all about the question: "What do you want?"

If you had Jesus right in front of you and he asked you, "What do you want?" what would you say to him? What are you asking God for? What is driving you? If you were that blind man, you'd give the same answer he did. You would start with your deepest longing—the dream that seems too good to be true, the dream that seems too good to come true.

Your dreams are a product of your longings. The dreams that fuel your life are fueled by your desires, by your passions, by your cravings. They're the things that burn inside you that if you cannot attain or accomplish, you feel like you would rather die.

I think a lot of us are like Bartimaeus, except we are going to Jesus and saying, "Lord, could you give me sight in one eye?" instead of, "Lord, could you give me twenty-twenty vision? I want to see." Is it possible that you are not living the life of your dreams because God has asked you what you want and you are asking for way too little? Have you been willing to settle for much less than your dream?

When I was in college, I got hit in a soccer match and injured my knee badly enough to send me to the hospital. (The hospital is sort of a theme in my life.) I was in a lot of pain when I got back to my apartment that night. My roommate had built a loft for our beds; he slept on one side, and I slept on the other side. And that night I was in so much pain that in the middle the night I literally rolled out of bed, fell out of the loft, and landed on top of an army surplus locker. Those things are really well built.

When I hit that locker, my arm snapped. I hit the corner of the locker with the full weight of my body pressed against my elbow, and I felt it surrender to the force of the collision.

My roommate, who was specializing in sports medicine, never even got out of bed. He asked, "Erwin, is that you?"

I said, "Oh, yeah, it's me," as I moaned in pain.

"Are you okay?"

"I don't think so. I think I need to go to the hospital."

He said, "No, no, just lie there."

He left me there all night. This is another theme in my life.

I said, "Well, I need some Tylenol or something."

"No, I don't think it's good to give you medicine."

So I lay there all night without anything to alleviate the pain. I had chills and sweats and chills and sweats. I was fighting trauma and shock all night. In the morning I was taken to the hospital after lying on the floor for five or six hours. The doctors took, if I remember correctly, more than twenty X-rays, trying to find all the things that might be broken.

I was informed that I damaged the radial head of my right elbow and would likely never regain mobility in my arm. My elbow was stuck at a forty-five-degree angle, and I had *zero* mobility. I began physical therapy with sports medicine, but my progress came to nothing—no movement in any direction.

Then I got an unexpected phone call from someone in Canada who was putting on an event, some kind of Woodstock-type thing. He asked me if I would come and play some of my music—I used to pretend to be a musician back then. I remember telling the guy that I just broke my arm and the doctors told me I would never be able to move it again.

Then I added, "Sure."

The guy said, "What?"

I said, "I'll be there. I'll play."

After I hung up the phone, I took a guitar, put it on my lap, and said, "God, would you move my hand from here to here so I can play?" I can't explain this to you, but instantly my arm went from being stuck in one spot to being stuck in another. I was like, *Wow! Now that was a stupid prayer.*

What do you want?

"Oh, I'd like to be able to see a little bit."

"I'd like a new coat."

"I'd like to walk with only a slight limp."

"Oh, I'd like my arm to move forty degrees south and be stuck there for the rest of my life."

It occurred to me that maybe if God healed me this much, maybe he would just go ahead and heal me the whole way.

I think a lot of our prayers make God wonder why we think so little of him. I can just imagine God looking at us and asking us, "What do you want?" Then he shakes his head and thinks, *If I could just get you to believe more, to care more, to want more than you're asking for.*

The problem with so much of the faith language we hear on the small screen is that it's all about getting more for us. When is enough, enough? There is nothing wrong with having things. The problem is that it misses the whole point. This isn't about asking for more stuff. Heaven help us if we still think that's what living wide awake is all about.

Living wide awake is about realizing that the world needs you to live up to your potential. There are others whose lives and future depend on you stepping up and living big. The better world you keep waiting for needs you to accept your life's calling and responsibility, and then to create it. The future needs you to dream God-sized dreams; these are the only kind God gets involved in. And if the future needs anything, it is God working through people.

WHO WILL YOU BECOME?

Another story in the Bible tells about the life of a young man named Joseph. If you know Broadway, you know Joseph. He's the guy with the multicolored coat. He was metro way before it was fashionable.

In Genesis 37, we are introduced to Joseph's character:

When Joseph was seventeen years old, he often tended his father's flocks with his half brothers, the sons of his father's wives Bilhah and Zilpah. But Joseph reported to his father some of the bad things his brothers were doing. Now Jacob loved Joseph more than any of his other children because Joseph had been born to him in his old age. So one day he gave Joseph a special gift—a beautiful robe. But his brothers hated Joseph because of their father's partiality. They couldn't say a kind word to him.

One night Joseph had a dream and promptly reported the details to his brothers, causing them to hate him even more. "Listen to this dream," he announced. "We were out in the field tying up bundles of grain. My bundle stood up, and then your bundles all gathered around and bowed low before it!"

You can just hear him. "What do you think that dream means, you guys?"

His brothers understood.

"So you are going to be our king, are you?" they taunted. And they hated him all the more for his dream and what he had said.

Then Joseph had another dream and told his brothers about it. "Listen to this dream," he said. "The sun, moon, and eleven stars bowed low before me!"

Interesting dream, isn't it?

This time [Joseph] told his father as well as his brothers, and his father rebuked him. "What do you mean?" his father asked. "Will your mother, your brothers, and I actually come and bow before you?" But while his brothers were jealous of Joseph, his father gave it some thought and wondered what it all meant.

Here's a little bit of advice: even if you are pondering a dream given to you by God, don't go telling everyone. This was not too bright on Joseph's part. If God gives you a dream for your life, it will come to pass if you choose to courageously pursue it, not because you become a salesman for it.

God gives God-sized dreams to people with God-shaped hearts. I think Joseph made a terrible mistake telling his brothers. His immaturity created a relational divide and provoked huge jealousy. But that doesn't discount that God was the one giving Joseph the dream. Part of the way God works in us is he begins to give us dreams of the lives we could live or the people we could become if we would trust him and live courageously. While his brothers despised Joseph and did everything they could to destroy his dreams, we find in his story the reminder that once you have a dream from God and refuse to relinquish it, that dream is going to come to pass no matter what opposition you face.

Joseph's brothers sold him into slavery, and he lived as a slave in Egypt. He served one of Pharaoh's officials and brought him tremendous success. His master's wife kept trying to seduce him, but due to his integrity he refused her advances. Angry at being scorned, the wife falsely accused Joseph of trying to rape her, and he was thrown into prison.

Years later, Joseph helped a guy in jail find his way to freedom. The prisoner promised to help Joseph, but he forgot him the moment he was free. Joseph continued to live his life as a slave and a prisoner.

Then after years of nothing but bad luck, Joseph caught a break because Pharaoh had a dream no one could interpret. This was Joseph's specialty, so he found freedom by unwrapping the Egyptian king's disturbing vision of the future. Through this, Joseph was given the position of chief adviser to Pharaoh. What must have felt like a lifetime later, Joseph was the most powerful man in Egypt, second only to Pharaoh.

This process in Joseph's life took not days or months or even years, but decades.

Sometimes the life God dreams
for us takes a lifetime to come to pass.
Great lives that are born out of great dreams
often come through great sacrifice and
great suffering.

Our dreams, the ones God places inside us, are a foretaste of our destiny. But there is a danger of wanting that dream so badly that you're willing to sacrifice your character. God will never sacrifice who you are for what you can accomplish. We are in danger when "getting there" becomes the most important thing to us. Even when you have the right dream, you can make the wrong choices.

The way you begin to live out your God-given dreams is to become the person God desires you to be. Joseph went on a long journey and he went through a lot of pain, and his life was a nightmare, but his dream was a foretaste of his destiny. Maybe the problem wasn't about how long it took for the dream to come to pass, but how long it took to make the dreamer.

Your dreams are
the product of your longings,
a portrait of your potential,
and a promise of your future.

Your dreams are God's way of whispering into your soul, *There's more to you than you know. There's more available to you than you can imagine. There's an extraordinary life awaiting you if you would trust me.*

But the question is, what can you see? Are you living a nightmare or lost in a fantasy because you're afraid there's nothing meaningful inside you? Are you paralyzed because you don't really believe God made you extraordinary and has planned for you a future worth getting up for?

Can you see who God has made you to become?

I think that's why community is so important. Sometimes we are blind to ourselves. We are afraid people might see inside us and conclude that we have no value at all. Often our fear or our sense of inadequacy is masked by arrogance and indifference. You were created in the image and likeness of God. As broken, damaged, and messed up as you may be, God sees extraordinary capacity in you. He'd love to be able to inform your dreams with the future that is coming if you would follow him. A dream needs a person to bring it to life. What kind of person do you need to become for your dream to come to life?

WHAT ARE YOU TO EMBRACE?

There was one moment in time where the lives of two men intersected and forever changed the course of history. Their names were Cornelius and Peter. We find them in the tenth chapter of the book of Acts.

Peter has become the leader of the movement that would soon become known as Christianity, and God has selected him to take the gospel to the Gentiles—everyone who is not a Jew. But this is outside of Peter's field of vision and sphere of concern. You can understand why. Peter is Jewish; he loves his people; he understands what it means to be Jewish; he's most comfortable in a Jewish world.

God hears the prayers of a Roman named Cornelius, who is crying out to him. Cornelius is doing all he knows to do to find God. He's caring for the poor and serving people, sincere in his pursuit, yet he has not found what he is looking for. God sees Cornelius's heart and wants Cornelius to know him. But guess what? Cornelius is not a Jew. This puts Cornelius out of Peter's field of vision or concern. No one who is a follower of Jesus Christ cares about this Roman man—yet.

God speaks to Cornelius through an angel, who tells Cornelius that God is going to send a man named Peter. Well, technically, he says that Cornelius will have to go get Peter. Through Peter, God is going to give this Roman man the life-changing message of what his Son, Jesus, has done. Yet the whole of it remains a mystery waiting for Peter to get there.

Now, Peter is spending some time praying as the story unfolds.

The next day as Cornelius's messengers were nearing the city, Peter went up to the flat roof to pray. It was about noon, and he was hungry. But while lunch was being prepared, he fell into a trance. He saw the sky open, and something like a large sheet was let down by its four corners. In the sheet were all sorts of animals, reptiles, and birds. Then a voice said to him, "Get up, Peter; kill and eat them."

"Never, Lord," Peter declared. "I have never in all my life eaten anything forbidden by our Jewish laws."

The voice spoke again, "If God says something is acceptable, don't say it isn't." The same vision was repeated three times. Then the sheet was pulled up again to heaven.

Peter was very perplexed. What could the vision mean? Just then the men sent by Cornelius found the house and stood outside at the gate. They asked if this was the place where Simon Peter was staying. Meanwhile, as Peter was puzzling over the vision, the Holy Spirit said to him, "Three men have come looking for you.

Go down and go with them without hesitation. All is well, for I have sent them."

For Peter, there are things that are clean and things that are unclean, only certain animals that the Hebrew Scriptures specified you can eat. These practices are an important part of Peter's faith and culture. This is at the core of what makes you a good and sincere Jew. If you eat the wrong things, you are unclean and defiled.

As Peter starts praying, he's really hungry. But believe me, he's not hungry for anything he sees in his dream. A blanket comes down from heaven—it's a picnic! But on the picnic blanket, there is a very unappealing menu.

Since it was Cornelius the Roman coming, it might have been Italian food—seafood pasta! And God is saying, *I want you to eat Italian. You just want to eat Jewish. There are some clams next to that baked ziti. I want you to eat them, Peter.* And Peter is probably thinking, *Give me lentils. I want my lox and bagels.* And God is saying, *No, Peter. Whatever I tell you is not unclean, you don't call it unclean; you eat it. You value it.*

Now, it is critical we understand this dream isn't merely about food. What's happening here is that through Peter's dream, God is saying, *Peter, your vision is too small. I am expanding your field of vision. I am broadening your sphere of concern. I am deepening the burden of your responsibility.*

Whenever God gives you a dream, he raises the bar. God isn't simply trying to inspire you but to call you to a more heroic life. When you invite God to give you a dream for your life, you will find God expanding the parameters of your concern. The apostle James tells us that if we know the right thing to do and do not do it, that is sin (James 4:17). Once the dream is in your heart, it is in your hands.

Peter's vision would prove to be more than he could have ever imagined. That's what happens when God invades your dreams. I'm from El Salvador, and if my dream became to reach everyone from my homeland, that would be about five million of us. That's a lot of people. At Mosaic, we are committed to serving everyone in the entire Los Angeles region—that's more than sixteen million people. People might say "That's a little ambitious, don't you think?" The answer is, yes, of course it is. Ambition advances every good cause when it becomes vision fueled by burden. Great dreams are the fuel for great ambition and great accomplishments.

God is saying to Peter, *You have a vision for all the people of Israel, and it's way too small. You can't focus on something as small as a nation when the world needs you. I want you, Peter, to expand the boundaries of your concern and deepen the burden of your responsibility. Call nothing and no one unclean. Everyone matters. Cornelius has a dream. His dream will become reality when your dream grows bigger. You are a part of each other's futures. Everything is connected. Now go and connect the dots.*

So Peter goes with the men from Joppa to see Cornelius. He realizes Cornelius is searching for God. It was outside of Peter's imagination that a person who was not a Jew could actually be genuinely seeking God. But his mind is changed forever.

I wonder, is your dream too small because your concern is too small? Is it time to listen to what God is saying to your heart and answer the question, *What am I to embrace?*

Why would professional educators move to Indonesia to serve the underserved where they would perhaps be unappreciated, uninvited, and unwanted? Why would an entrepreneur and his wife from the French Riviera move their family to Morocco to serve in Muslim communities where education and opportunity are often considered a threat? Why would a concert pianist go into the remotest villages of Turkey to build houses and work as an educator for Kurds? Why would a couple from North Carolina move to Senegal to work in impoverished African communities? Is it possible that when we begin to find the dream for our lives, it always involves helping others live their dreams?

It is impossible to live in LA and be unaware of the influence of L. Ron Hubbard and Scientology. It seems more than coincidence that as I was writing this chapter I received this quote by Hubbard through my trusty BlackBerry: "A culture is only as great as its dreams, and its dreams are dreamed by artists." I could not agree more with Hubbard on the first part of this observation. And I couldn't agree less with the second. For a culture to become truly great, we must all begin to dream—not only our artists, but also our nurses and teachers, our fathers and mothers, our children and our elderly, our poor and our prosperous. We all can become dreamers; we all must become dreamers. After all, a life well lived is the most exquisite work of art. So perhaps yes, it is true that the future is created by the dreams of our artists, if we accept that we are all in fact artists. The artist is the hero waiting to be awakened within you.

As we begin to create the life of our dreams, we must answer for ourselves perhaps the most critical question that will direct and shape our future—*what are you to embrace?* This is a question of passion and compassion. The answer will determine the world that you will change. Great dreams begin as we expand our concern and deepen our burden and muster our courage and begin to live. You cannot even begin to live the dream God has for you until you stop caring about only yourself. And the smaller your span of concern, the smaller your dream will be and the smaller your life will become. God had to speak to Peter in a dream so Peter could live the life of his dreams. Your dreams create space for the dreams of others.

WHAT MUST YOU FACE?

If you're going to create the life of your dreams, you're going to need to dream big so you can live big. Your life will never become what you do not dare to imagine. You will not become everything you dream of, but you'll never become anything you don't dream of. And when you begin to dream, guess what happens—your dreams are soon invaded by nightmares. As soon as you begin to dream, all the things you're afraid of start haunting you. Doubts, insecurities, the secret things no one else knows start popping into your dreams and can turn them into nightmares in a moment.

There's a moment in the history of Israel where they felt they had no hope. They believed in God, but they didn't believe God could fix their situation. Have you ever been there? Have you been in those moments? You believe in God, you believe in the Bible, you believe in Jesus, but your life is a mess. You think, *I'm a shipwreck. I've absolutely destroyed any potential of ever living the life of my dreams.*

At times like this, you might be best described as nothing but dead bones. You're just waiting to be put six feet under. Your flesh in your muscle hasn't decayed, but your soul decayed a long time ago. And it may be that God is asking you a question like he asked the prophet Ezekiel generations ago.

The LORD took hold of me, and I was carried away by the Spirit of the LORD to a valley filled with bones. He led me around among the old, dry bones that covered the valley floor. They were scattered everywhere across the ground. Then he asked me, "Son of man, can these bones become living people again?"

"O Sovereign LORD," I replied, "you alone know the answer to that."

Then he said to me, "Speak to these bones and say, 'Dry bones, listen to the word of the LORD! This is what the Sovereign LORD says: Look! I am going to breathe into you and make you live again! I will put flesh and muscles on you and cover you with skin. I will put breath into you, and you will come to life. Then you will know that I am the LORD.'"

So I spoke these words, just as he told me. Suddenly as I spoke, there was a rattling noise all across the valley. The bones of each body came together and attached themselves as they had been before. Then as I watched, muscles and flesh formed over the bones. Then skin formed to cover their bodies, but they still had no breath in them.

I think many of us have a life that is a dream still not yet completed.

We're in a dream half-baked, half-lived, half-accomplished.
We got really close and it didn't happen so we gave up.
We gave up on living the life of our dreams.
Then he said to me, "Speak to the winds." (v. 9)

Right.
Speak to the winds.
Sure.
Every day the wind does what I say. It's amazing.

"Speak to the winds and say: 'This is what the Sovereign LORD says: Come, O breath, from the four winds!'"

I've never controlled one wind.
Now I'm going to control all four.

"Breathe into these dead bodies so they may live again."
    So I spoke as he commanded me, and the wind entered the bodies and they began to breathe. They all came to life and stood up on their feet—a great army of them.

Some dreams are so powerful you cannot let them rest in your sleep.
You have to live them when you're awake.
You dream with your eyes open.

Then he said to me, "Son of man, these bones represent the people of Israel. They are saying, 'We have become old, dry bones-all hope is gone.' Now give them this message from the Sovereign LORD: O my people, I will open your graves of exile and cause you to rise again. Then I will bring you back to the land of Israel. When this happens, O my people, you will know that I am the LORD. I will put my Spirit in you, and you will live and return home to your own land. Then you will know that I am the LORD. You will see that I have done everything just as I promised. I, the LORD, have spoken!"

ARE YOU READY TO LIVE?

Maybe you've messed up an endless number of times. You've said to God, "This time I'm going to get it right. I'm serious. I'm going to do it." And as soon as you came out of the gate, you came crashing down and, in your mind, you are nothing but dry old bones. You can't even find your grave.

God wants to ask you one more question: can these dead bones live?

What must you face? What fears haunt you? What failures have marked you? What darkness has consumed you and stolen from you, robbed from you, sucked out of your soul the dream God created you to flesh out? Maybe there's a dream buried deep inside your soul, and God is waiting to reconstruct it, to put all the bones back together. He is waiting to put muscle and sinew on it and wrap skin around it.

God is waiting for you to recognize that you cannot control the four winds, but he can. If he commands you to act, and if you will trust him, you will see all of creation move in concert to accomplish in you what you were created to do. You were created not to simply sleep through your dreams but to live dreams bigger than you, bolder than you.

What do you want?

Who are you to become?

What will you embrace?

What must you face?

Are you ready to live?

Your dreams are a foretaste of the life you can have and the person you can become. But before you'll ever live those dreams, you have to discover a dream worth living. That's why God is so essential to this journey and why Jesus has come for us. Long before you took your first breath, you were a dream—a dream in the mind of the one who made you. He saw you before you were created, and he alone knows the full extent of your creative potential.

He sees the dream that could become your life. A life beyond your wildest dreams. Don't take your last breath without living it. It may seem like a contradiction in terms, but to live your dreams you have to live wide awake. The moment you start living wide awake, you begin to dream of a world waiting to exist. You become an artist.

Dreams are your palette but life is your canvas! You dream and imagine a future yet to be created. More than twenty years ago I began my work as a futurist. Not the kind who simply gets a glimpse of what tomorrow could look like, but the kind who shapes what tomorrow will look like. It was Victor Hugo who once wrote, "There is nothing like a dream to create the future." This is the artistry for which you were created.

So awaken and dream—then create the future.

discover 2

THE EXPLORER

WE WERE IN AN OPEN JEEP IN THE NORTHERN TIP OF South Africa on a pitch-black night, surrounded by wild lions. (I guess you don't have to add *wild* to *lion*, do you?) Later we would find a pair of rhinos, a bull elephant, and an endless array of other African wildlife. That morning, we had taken a walking safari in the very places we sat quietly among the king of the beasts. It had not been long since two photographers were mauled on their expedition. Somehow that only added to heighten our senses.

For us, this is a family vacation. Mariah was fourteen, and Aaron seventeen. It has always been my wife Kim's dream to serve in Africa. Now she has explored the continent from South Africa to Senegal to Zambia. She has literally done Africa from A to Z. Kim has always had an adventurer's spirit, so it is no surprise to anyone who knows her that she wants to live in what has been known as the Dark Continent. She was passionate about Africa long before it became the center of global attention. I have followed her there. Now I find myself in Africa more than I am in Atlanta. My dreams have grown because of it. And when you begin to dream, you begin to explore.

It's an inescapable reality that if we're going to live the life of our dreams, it's going to take courage, willingness to risk, to attempt, to fail, to get back up. To live a life bigger than ourselves requires going beyond words or even thoughts; this kind of life has to be created in our imaginations. And our imaginations must be continuously fueled by an insatiable curiosity.

CHILDLIKE CURIOSITY

Once you are willing and ready to dream, then you are ready to move to the next phase of living wide awake. To begin to live out your dreams, you must begin to explore.

Just as you have been uniquely created by God to dream and imagine, you are also designed to learn, to discover, to invent. One of the things that gets lost along the way is a unique gift each of us has from childhood—we all are born with not only imagination, but also curiosity.

You don't have to teach children how to be curious. You don't even have to fuel or inspire their curiosity. Every child is naturally curious—insatiably curious, dangerously curious, maybe even irritatingly curious. You don't have to tell a child to explore, to touch, to feel, to look, to eat. You have to watch children every minute because they're going places they're not supposed to go, trying things they're not supposed to try, and getting themselves in all kinds of trouble.

George Bernard Shaw once mused that youth is wasted on the young. Einstein, on the other hand, posed that imagination is more important than knowledge. I wonder if it isn't a combination of the two that is most poignant—imagination is wasted on the young. Einstein was proof of the power of a childlike curiosity in the hands of an adult human being. We readily connect knowledge to maturity. Curiosity unfortunately is far too often relegated to the place of a childhood luxury. Our passion for discovery and exploration becomes another victim of growing up. We try so hard to break ourselves free of all of the constraints and limitations of childhood, moving into rebellion in our teenage years because we want to be free. We want to grow up; we want to be adults; we want to be mature. Yet the tragedy is that the things we should keep with us, the things that make us unique and allow us to turn our dreams into reality, we give up as we strive so desperately to grow up.

We lose our imagination and our curiosity. We stop exploring. I think if we were honest with ourselves, many of us have put our curiosities to rest. Because after all, curiosity killed the cat, and you're trying to survive. Maybe you didn't really get the best response from being curious. Looking back and asking questions may have worn thin when the answers never seemed to satisfy your thirst for knowledge. Maybe your curiosity, all the times you asked why, drove your parents out of their minds and they told you to hush or finally resorted to the old standby: "Because I told you so." And they begin establishing boundaries for your curiosity because they got tired of fueling it.

Maybe our curiosity led us to places that were destructive. You didn't get killed, but you were close to proving that curiosity really does kill or at least leaves you significantly injured. And so you started being less curious. Or maybe you found a way to pay the bills; you were able to get that eight-to-five job, pay the rent, and put gas in the car. Even though it's harder to live without exploring, and you feel the life being sucked out of you by the mundane, you stop being curious simply because your life is manageable. So you give up your insatiable curiosity in exchange for comfort and security and predictability.

But if you're going to create the life of your dreams, you have to once again choose to explore. You need to make it a life mandate to learn everything and anything you need to know to turn your dreams into reality. You have to start making yourself flexible and pliable again, because if you stop learning, you will stop growing and will never create a life beyond the one you have right now.

It's like languages. Have you ever tried to learn a language? Especially when you are older than, say, sixteen? I have. I've dabbled. I get inspired. I moved to LA sixteen years ago, and I started meeting many people from China. So I thought I'd learn Chinese. It can't be that hard to learn Chinese, right? I started with a few simple phrases—standard stuff, like *hello, good-bye,* and *thank you.* So I would go to a Chinese restaurant and try to impress the waiter, and then he would politely explain, "No, that's Cantonese; I speak Mandarin." She speaks Cantonese; he speaks Mandarin. The waiter over there doesn't speak either—he speaks a tribal dialect from somewhere else deep in China. And I'm like, "When you guys decide to learn one language, I'll jump back in." So I moved on from Chinese, because it was Greek to me.

Then I went to Japan. Oh, I love Japanese culture. The whole samurai thing is incredibly compelling. (Ever seen *Ghost Dog? The Last Samurai? Seven Samurai?*) It seemed so easy; the language sounds kind of like my native Spanish. And surely passion would close the gap where talent lets me down. There I was again—*hello, good-bye,* and *thank you.* Soon after that I was like, "You guys use a lot of syllables. There's got to be an easier way."

Then I went to Korea. I love the Korean people, so I decided to learn some Korean. This time I got past the big three phrases and learned little things, like *My name is Erwin. This is my wife, Kim.* (By the way, Kim is a good Korean name—if it were her last name.) I learned important things. *Where is the bathroom? No kimchi, please*—things like that. But then after a while, I hit the wall again.

Oh, if I could just become a child again. When I was little, I learned a new language and mastered it. I remember when I first heard English. It was just a bunch of sounds, a bunch of noise, and I couldn't understand what anyone was saying. They say it's very difficult to learn English. But piece by piece, as I listened to the sounds and struggled my way through it, the sounds started connecting to meaning, and noise started connecting to things, events, people. And before I knew it, I learned English, which is no small thing for a kid from El Salvador who spoke Spanish as his first language.

I had learned Spanish by age two. It was so easy, so simple. English was a little harder, but I picked that up pretty quickly. Spanish at two years old, and English at five years old—I had so much momentum. What happened to me? Simply put, my brain grew up. Oh, to have the mind of a child.

INSATIABLE LEARNERS

The longer we live, the less pliable our minds are to learning. And certainly that is going to be our epitaph if we give up on learning, if we think we've learned enough, or if we've chosen to simply work off what we know. We convince ourselves that somehow what we already know will take us where we need to go. Unfortunately, we who build our lives on the Scriptures are at times most in danger when we conclude all we need to know is in one book so we can be ignorant of everything else.

A person of faith must never be afraid to explore. We above all others should be driven to question, to examine, to learn. Faith shouldn't make you less curious but insatiably curious. When you live in relationship to the God of all creation, learning is a given. You are now and forever on a journey involving mystery and discovery. This journey is as endless as God is infinite and eternal. For all eternity we will be not only worshippers but also explorers.

You were created by God to explore, to discover, to define, to learn, to invent, to pioneer. All the way back in the beginning, you see this in the Scriptures. In the early chapters of Genesis, we find an encounter between God and the first man, Adam:

> And the LORD God said, "It is not good for the man to be alone. I will make a companion who will help him." So the LORD God formed from the soil every kind of animal and bird. He brought them to Adam to see what he would call them, and Adam chose a name for each one. He gave names to all the livestock, birds, and wild animals. But still there was no companion suitable for him.

The overarching story in this passage is that God is preparing man to realize he needs woman—that together they will make humanity. The process God uses, though, is what I want us to focus on here. God tells Adam to name all the animals on the earth—all the livestock, all the birds, all the wild animals. Just stop and think about that. It tells us something about the way God created you. You have an unlimited learning capacity. How many of us even know all the animals on the earth? I don't. Do you?

Just the fact that Adam could name all the birds is amazing. I know a hummingbird when I see one. After that, it gets all blurry. Pigeons are just overweight and unattractive doves to me. I can hardly tell the difference between a crow and a raven. Can you? What really is the difference except ravens are British and crows are American? I don't know. How about between a swallow and a mockingbird? But Adam names all the birds. This tells us not only that hewas inventive in the naming process, but that he had the ability to distinguish between every species and identify the uniqueness of each one. That's amazing. He started from scratch. He was learning as he went. And he had an unlimited learning capacity.

And Adam could identify all the reptiles—it would be really important for the survival of the species to distinguish between venomous and nonvenomous snakes. Just this summer, my twelve-year-old nephew, Lucas, who loves snakes, was handling a copperhead, and it struck him in the hand. He is really skilled at something most of us consider anything but child's play. Lucas has no fear and is endlessly curious when it comes to reptiles. It is impossible to keep him from his passion when he lives in Florida, where humans keep encroaching on the wildlife. Having handled snakes many times before, he just calmly put the copperhead in a jar and took it with him to the emergency room.

Someone more knowledgeable than me, like my nephew, might insist, "Don't kill it. It's not dangerous." I'm in the "If it slithers, it's the enemy" camp.

There are coral snakes that are red and white and black. There are also king snakes that look like coral snakes but are not poisonous. Coral snakes, by the way, are very poisonous. You have to get close enough to notice the black boundary around the design, and then you know it's not a coral snake, so it's harmless. If Adam is the only human being on the planet, I don't want him getting anywhere near a coral snake and trying to figure out which one is harmless and which one is lethal. He not only named them, but he could distinguish between them.

There are people who can identify every one of these different species. I grew up near the Everglades in Miami, so I know the difference between a crocodile and an alligator. I can tell by the shape of the snout, and I know crocodiles can open their mouths with both jaws and alligators only with one, and things like that. But really if you're Adam, do you want to get close enough to discover the difference between an alligator and a crocodile? Just name them as a general category; stay away.

Human beings have an unlimited learning capacity. You've been designed by God to learn. Now it doesn't mean that you can learn everything that is out there, but it means that you can learn everything you need to know to properly inform your dreams. Curiosity is essential for life. Curiosity is essential for learning. Curiosity keeps you exploring.

To live the life God created you to live, you must continue to explore. It's a part of the way God designed you. That's why when we're children, we have an insatiable curiosity, a need to discover, and a drive to explore. It's a part of the way God made us.

A Curious Legacy

If you stop exploring; you stop growing. In fact, if children were not curious, they would not develop the skills to survive. Do you recognize that part of the reason you ask questions, the reason you need to know, the reason you are even capable of learning, is because God designed you with this extraordinary capacity? He gave you the capacity to learn, to grow, to understand.

But it's more than that. It's that life is an incredible journey, an extraordinary adventure. As you move forward in your life, you're going to face obstacles and challenges and problems. As children, our drive to learn is simply an expression of being human; in our adulthood, learning is an expression of humility. And if you do not have the character to keep learning, you will limit your capacity to keep advancing. If we were incapable of learning, we would never grow or change.

We are first dreamers, then explorers. In Genesis 4, we find some of our early ancestors. Verse 20 says, "Adah gave birth to a baby named Jabal. He became the first of the herdsmen who lived in tents." Before him, no herdsmen lived in tents.

Now imagine what it was like when it was raining. It was wet and uncomfortable, and they probably all ran under trees, and the ones who had the leafier trees were drier in the morning. And after a while they thought, *We should probably camp under trees when it looks like it's going to rain.* Eventually this guy named Jabal thought, *There isn't always a tree around, and not all the trees are always in bloom, and there are bad winters, cold and wet and leafless.* Maybe with a few skins and pelts around, he started connecting them together. Piece by piece he created the first tent. Can you imagine how all the other herdsmen were burning with envy? There they were getting soaked out in the rain, and there was Jabal underneath his tent. He was the first to live in a tent.

And his brother's name was Jubal. Now Jubal appreciated the tent, I'm sure, but he was more of an artisan. Genesis 4:21 says, he was "the first musician—the inventor of the harp and flute." So before Jubal there was no harp and flute—perhaps even no instruments at all. His innovation accentuated everyone's capacity to enjoy, to celebrate and worship.

A harp may not be as practical as a tent, but it may contribute far more to the human experience. A flute might not keep you dry at night, but it may do more to keep you alive in the morning. A tent brings you shelter; music reaches into your soul. There are moments when one will be far more important to us than the other, which is a great reminder that we all have a contribution to make.

Verse 22 tells us, "To Lamech's other wife, Zillah, was born Tubal-Cain. He was the first to work with metal, forging instruments of bronze and iron." So before Tubal-Cain, there was bronze and iron lying around everywhere without any value whatsoever. And then maybe Tubal-Cain saw someone get eaten by a bear. And he realized, *I have a disadvantage.* The bear has claws, so he took a piece of iron and he made claws for himself and called it a spear. Who knows? Maybe he saw some problem that needed to be overcome. Maybe he created armor so that the bear claws wouldn't cut into his chest on the first stroke. But whatever the case was, Tubal-Cain realized he had some material, iron and bronze, that had untapped potential.

How many of us are living unaware of all the unused potential around us? Or even within us? Maybe your life is defined by problems you have not yet overcome, and you've conceded that these are your limitations and boundaries. Throughout history, people have faced challenges, obstacles, and problems that seemed insurmountable to everyone but one. One person found a way to overcome the problem that all the rest deemed insurmountable. Once solved, everyone sees it. You don't find people who choose not to live in tents after tents are invented. Once you start forging the bronze and the iron, everyone wants the bronze and the iron. And by the way, it seems everyone loves some good music too.

Our drive to explore has not only changed the human experience, but it has changed the course of human history. It was *Apollo 11* astronaut Michael Collins who said, "Exploration is not a choice, really; it is an imperative." For those of us who have been able to sustain a sense of wonder and curiosity as adults, it seems there is no limit to our capacity to explore, or at least to our curiosity. Give us a problem, and we become determined to solve it, not to mention how motivated we become when it's a mystery.

There are those who think their intelligence should be solely focused on identifying problems. Have you ever been around people who think their contribution to the team is only to point out the impossibilities? These people think they are geniuses. You are sitting in the room, and everyone is dreaming, planning, envisioning, imagining; then one of these people points out everything that will go wrong. He assumes no one has seen these problems. His only contribution is to identify everything that isn't working and explaining why nothing can be done about it. In the minds of these people, you are not allowed to dream great dreams, to make the problems seem incidental.

If the wall is the limitation, how smart do you have to be to realize there's a wall there? Once you run into it two or three times, you might say, "There's a wall here." Real genius, real invention, is not about identifying a problem but about solving it.

Wouldn't it be wonderful if, when we saw a problem, we assumed we were to be part of the solution? Seeing a problem only lets you know where your limits are if you don't solve it. Problems, obstacles, and challenges can either become the markers of our limits and limitations, or they can become the springboard into a whole new world.

The Bible tells us that right away, from the very beginning of human history, there were men and women who were creative and inventive; they were explorers. With each and every new solution, they would soon find a new and challenging problem. But they kept finding a solution to that problem. They were problem solvers, and the world was never the same because of them.

Which, by the way, is one of the mantras in my own life. There are times when I face an obstacle, a challenge, a problem that seems so big it's overwhelming. And I tell myself, *I only need one more solution than I have problems.* If you keep finding one more solution than your problems, then you can keep moving forward.

Maybe what you need right now is to recognize God created you to be adaptable and expandable. No matter how big your obstacles or challenges are, God created you to find a solution to overcome them. Now I know some of us love spiritualizing things, as in, "Well, God will solve the problem." But God rarely solves the problem with people who just say, "If God wants it solved, he'll do it." Instead, he seems to solve the problem with people who don't give up. Have you ever noticed that?

THE GREAT EXPLORERS

God seems to free the oppressed, end injustice, feed the hungry, bring victory, and do every good work through men and women who refuse to surrender to the problem. As we move ahead on our spiritual journey, we discover that we have to once again become explorers. If you choose not to believe in God or even reject mystery in any form, maybe it would make sense to stop exploring things. However, if you are in a relationship with Jesus Christ, you are an explorer whether you like it or not. Once you are called out by God, you are called to move into mysterious, uncertain territories and to begin to live a life filled with risk and fraught with challenges.

Remember how God called out Abram?

Then the LORD told Abram, "Leave your country, your relatives, and your father's house, and go to the land that I will show you. I will cause you to become the father of a great nation. I will bless you and make you famous, and I will make you a blessing to others.

I will bless those who bless you and curse those who curse you. All the families of the earth will be blessed through you."

So Abram departed as the LORD had instructed him, and Lot went with him. Abram was seventy-five years old when he left Haran. He took his wife, Sarai, his nephew Lot, and all his wealth—his livestock and all the people who had joined his household at Haran-and finally arrived in Canaan.

One thing I love about this particular story is that if you ever feel like you can't keep learning, that you're too old to explore, you can just think of Abram. Abram was seventy-five years old, so you can't tell me you're too old. He was seventy-five when God said, "Abram, I have an entirely new adventure for you." So it seems like retirement happens right about the moment you die when it comes to God. There is never a point in your life where you lack value or significance. There's always something for you to contribute.

God told Abram to leave his country, leave his relatives, leave his father's house, and go to a land God would show him. Just before that, we learn that "Terah took his son Abram, his daughter-in-law Sarai, his grandson Lot, his son Haran's child, and left Ur of the Chaldeans to go to the land of Canaan. But they stopped instead at the village of Haran and settled there."

So it seems that Terah was supposed to go to Canaan, but he did not. So his family settled in this other land. Now God is saying to Abram, "I need you to finish the journey."

I think a lot of us are where we are in our lives because this is just sort of where we got stuck. You didn't feel a God-inspired call to where you live; you just happened to be born there or transferred there. You are being manipulated by the circumstances of your life rather than being moved by a calling with purpose and mission.

When you are called out by God, you have to take on a learning mode that recognizes you are called by God to explore unknown territories and go to uncertain environments. To some of you, God is literally saying, *You need to leave your country, your relatives, your house and go to a place you've never known if you are going to live the life of your dreams.*

I wonder if you've just settled because this happens to be where you are. It's important to ask, why are you doing what you're doing? Do you have a career or a calling? Are you there by accident or by intention? I understand needing to pay the bills. I get that there are times and circumstances where the best you can do is to do your best at whatever you are doing. There are those who do well simply to make it through the day.

The question remains, though: are you living up to your calling? Are you maximizing your God-given opportunities? Abram was called out to greatness, and it changed not only his life but the lives of generations to come. Ironically, those who don't have the opportunity to live a life worth dreaming of need you to pursue great dreams for them. They need you to live up to your opportunity so they might have one. So you have a job? Great. It's the job you have, not the job you want. But the job you have is better than the job you don't have, so you settle for the job even though you don't want it. You just settle there, and you're miserable. But you're paralyzed by fear because you stopped growing, you stopped learning, you stopped exploring, you stopped discovering, and you stopped dreaming.

I wonder if some of you need to move to Tibet or maybe India or South America. Or maybe you need to find a way to deal with the issue of AIDS in Africa. Is it possible that to create the life of your dreams, you need to get up and leave what you know and relinquish the security of what you have in order to discover what you only see in your imagination? Remember, there is always a hero within you waiting to be awakened—that hero is the explorer.

I remember when Kim first went to China. I was invited to go to China about thirteen years ago, and I said, "Hold the spot for me." Then I went to Kim and said, "Honey, I always get to experience everything first, and then I come back and tell you about it. So I want you to take my spot going to China, and I want you to come back and tell me about it."

So she prepared and went to China, and she had a life-changing experience. She came back so moved. She said, "Honey, one day you have to go to a third world country." It might be hard to imagine, but back then, we thought of countries like China and India as underdeveloped. I said, "Honey, I'm from a third world country." She responded as if she were in an "Ah-ha" moment, "Oh yeah." she said to our foster daughter, Paty, "One day you've got to go." But Paty is from a third world country. And you know what is funny, I think sometimes it's only hard for Kim to remember that I am actually an immigrant because I am so at home here in the States.

Sometimes we think that if we leave everything we know, it's going to get worse from there. But it is possible you'll never find greater contentment or joy or exhilaration until you're willing to give up what you know and what you have for what awaits and exists in the unknown.

GOOD THINKING

You are created by God to be a pioneer, to explore unknown places and have uncertain experiences because he created and designed you to solve whatever challenges and problems and obstacles you will face in that place. When you live up to your greatness, the whole world is made better. The world cannot afford for you to choose *average* or *easy*. Don't let the routine of life put you in a rut. But I think there needs to be a warning: when I say you should learn everything, I don't mean you should experience everything. Not everything you need to know is meant to be learned through experience.

I know this way of thinking is very popular today. People say, "I have to experience it for myself. I have to learn it for myself." Know what it's called when you think you have to experience everything before you can actually know better? It's called stupidity.

Let's go back to Genesis 2. It says, "The LORD God placed the man in the Garden of Eden to tend and care for it. But the LORD God gave him this warning: 'You may freely eat any fruit in the garden except fruit from the tree of the knowledge of good and evil. If you eat of its fruit, you will surely die.'"

I hear people all the time say, "Well, that's your interpretation." How else do you interpret that? It's not complicated. "You eat from this tree, you die." It's very simple. Eat from any and all of the other trees, and you'll be fine. Eat freely, enjoy, and live. God says explore, discover, experience, enjoy, live. Eat any fruit you want; eat all of it you want. By the way, some of the fruits taste better peeled, but just go ahead. You'll figure that out. Some of them you eat the outside; some you only eat the inside. It's all going to be an adventure for you. Just don't eat from this one tree, the tree of knowledge of good and evil. If you eat from this tree, it will kill you."

Not everything you are to learn has to be learned by experience. Some things you should learn through the wisdom of others who have failed, and some things you should learn by having confidence in God and building your life on his shared wisdom.

If there's ever any proof that many of us can't learn except the hard way, it's the iron. If you were like me as a child, it wooed you—calling like a siren in the night. It begged to be touched, especially when that red light was on and it made that hissing sound. It was so attractive, so you waited until your mom was gone, and then you made your move.

You are an intelligent person. You had good parents. They told you not to touch the iron. They warned you that you would get burned. So maybe you avoided learning by personal experience on this one. But some of us had parents who said, "I love you, and I am going to let you have what you want." They didn't give us a lot of rules and boundaries. It would've been more compelling if they had said, "When you put your tiny little hand on that hot iron, your skin is going to melt off your bones."

The iron offers so many learning opportunities. After you brand your hand with that infamous triangle, you see the other end. What is that little plug? Where does it go? Why should it be the only one allowed to go into that exciting little socket in the wall? Other things should be allowed to go there, metal things, wet things. I wonder how many of us put something into an electrical socket? You would think the lot of us were orphans. It's as if we never had anyone to warn us: "Don't put anything into the socket. There's electricity there, and it's going to hurt you."

The truth is, we just decided we had to learn for ourselves. What we should learn from wisdom we insist on learning through the pain that comes from being unteachable (which is a nice way of saying we choose to be stupid). There are some things we either learn or we stop living. Other lessons have a subtler effect. It has been said that leaders are learners. This is because when you stop learning, you stop growing. When you stop growing, you start dying. You have moved from living to existing. It's not just that leaders are learners, but only learners are fully alive.

There are some things in life that if you experience them, they're going to destroy you. You can pretend that you're learning, but you're not. You're destroying the dream you were created to live. You've been told that if you keep spending time with that woman who's not your wife, eventually the relationship is going to go in the wrong direction. You've been warned if you commit adultery, you're going to lose the person you love the most and who loves you the most, but you decided you have to learn for yourself.

You've been warned. It's not like you've never heard it. You've been told that if you keep looking at Internet porn, you're going to become addicted and lose the capacity to have genuine intimacy with your spouse. You just don't believe it. It's not true about you. You've been told if you keep cutting corners, keep telling white lies and allowing other subtle dishonesties, that eventually your heart will become corrupt, and you will lose the capacity to tell the truth. Before you know it, you lose your career and your integrity, because you just had to learn for yourself.

You've been told that if you won't forgive, if you keep that bitterness in your heart, you can justify it by being righteous, but that anger is going to corrode your soul and you're going to lose the capacity to experience love and to treat the people you love with empathy. Your heart will grow cold from the anger and bitterness.

But it's like the iron. *What do they know?* you think. *They're really holding back. They're trying to keep us from an experience that would enhance our lives.* Do you really think God told Adam and Eve not to eat from that one tree because God was holding out on them? There are some things you are not supposed to learn from experience because the experience will kill you.

This insatiable curiosity inside us can lead us to destructive places. Every act of greed, every act of violence, every act of corruption is preceded by an imagination that went there long before. The world we create in our heads is the world we will create through our actions. The Internet is a popular way to extrovert the human imagination. We are quickly and sadly discovering how dark the human heart can be. What begins as curiosity can fast become corruption.

At first, it may appear that we can imagine things that bring out the worst of us without consequence. The consequence, though, is that when we dwell in dark places we eventually become consumed by the darkness.

The tension here, of course, is that a part of the wonder and power of a childlike imagination is that children have no fear of being wrong. And for us to grow and thrive we must be willing to fail.

PILGRIM'S PROGRESS

God placed inside you an insatiable curiosity. God made you to explore so that your pilgrimage would drive you to him. Your curiosity is a fuel from God to keep you searching and asking until you find him, and then to keep you searching and asking so you can know him.

One of the best examples of how this is played out is the life of Moses.

One day Moses was tending the flock of his father-in-law, Jethro, the priest of Midian, and he went deep into the wilderness near Sinai, the mountain of God. Suddenly, the angel of the LORD appeared to him as a blazing fire in a bush. Moses was amazed because the bush was engulfed in flames, but it didn't burn up. "Amazing!" Moses said to himself.

Now here it is. This is what motivated Moses to have a life-changing encounter with the living God. He asked, "Why isn't that bush burning up? I must go over to see this."

Moses sees a bush. It's on fire, but it's not burning up. He says, "Cool. I need to get a closer look." It was nothing more than his insatiable curiosity that drove Moses into the presence of God.

Has it ever occurred to you that you can't stop asking why? The reason you have this need to know, the reason you have an insatiable curiosity, a capacity to learn, a need to discover, is that God created you to search for him and to grow in him.

I have a friend who once said to me, "I can't wait until I go to heaven because then I'm going to get all of my questions answered. I just can't wait. I have so many questions to ask God." Have you ever felt that way?

I said, "What in the world made you think you're going to get all the answers?"

He said, "Well, I am, aren't I?" And he was turning white, very distraught.

I pointed out that the Bible doesn't say you're going to get all the answers. In fact, it never says you're going to know everything about God. It says you're going to know God. A more likely scenario is you step into eternity, and suddenly all your questions are overwhelmed by new ones. One second in the presence of the

Creator of the universe, and you're going to get a truckload of new questions.

Eternity isn't the place where you get all the answers. Eternity is a place where you get all new questions, a place where you will always be learning. God is infinite. How long does it take to get to know everything about an infinite God? Oh, I'd say, about eternity. You were designed by God to be curious and to learn. Part of this is God's desire to drive you to him, to keep you searching until you find the one who created you so you can know him intimately, so your life can be changed and your dreams can become a reality.

Keith Le, a PhD in biochemistry from UCLA, decided to trust Jesus Christ with his life, his dreams, and his future on April Fool's Day. From outside observation it must have seemed an incredibly foolish thing for a person as smart as him to do, but Keith knew he wasn't closing his mind but opening his heart. God really does have a sense of humor. He could have waited for April 2. Le's journey did not end that day but had only just begun. A man whose entire life has been about learning became an explorer.

This is how it begins for all of us who find the life God created us to live—we are all seekers who became dreamers, who became explorers. We are all pilgrims stepping into an unknown future. It is through our pilgrimage that each of us and, in fact, the world makes progress. We are each artists painting a picture of the world we will create. We are also explorers on a search for all we need for the journey and to face the challenges ahead.

Years ago, I was inspired to write a series of entries from a fable I called the *Perils of Ayden*. In one sequence, young Ayden was asking his mentor, Maven, if he was ready for the challenges he would face on his impending journey. He asked with great fear and apprehension, "Have I learned everything I need to know?"

Maven, with a great calm that came from his unshakable confidence in his student, simply replied, "You know everything you need to learn."

When you become an explorer, the pilgrimage begins.

adapt **3**

THE ALCHEMIST

HAVE YOU EVER HAD HUGE DREAMS AND IDEAS FOR a big life you know you were supposed to live, but you felt you were somehow ill equipped, improperly trained? Does it seem your inadequacies and insecurities negate all your opportunities and potential?

It was easier when we were young. We could just dream about or imagine anything. You're a kid, so there's no pressure to actually act on your dreams. Just having big dreams was enough to impress. Then you're in college, and you change your major five or six or twelve times and finish with a degree in general studies. Not the ideal, but it's still okay. You move from one job to another, you know, finding yourself.

In LA, where I live, you rarely meet anyone who is actually doing the job he or she came here to do. It seems everyone is in transition. No one is settled; everyone is striving to accomplish something else, to become someone more than he or she really is. I used to ask people, "What do you do?" I don't do that as much anymore. I've discovered it's a sore spot for a lot of people. "I'm just sort of working," they'll say. I think a lot of us have temporary jobs as we search for the career we really want. And it makes me wonder if it's a different career we are hoping for . . . or a different life.

You find professionals, people who actually have postgraduate degrees—MBAs, PhDs—and they have a midlife crisis at the age of twenty-seven. "I'm an engineer, but I really want to be a producer." Or, "I'm a doctor, but I want to do something meaningful with my life. I want to be a photographer." Or, "I'm a corporate lawyer, but I've always dreamed of being an author."

Have you ever had one of those conversations with someone? Or have you had one of those conversations in your own mind? No matter what kind of training you pursued, there's another dream that keeps haunting you. If your career path doesn't seem to match your heart's longing, it may be you have a skill that doesn't match your passion. You were good at something, so it seemed obvious that is what you should do. Or maybe it was a choice between career and family—and you always put others above yourself. You have no regrets, but you do have unfulfilled dreams.

You can't escape that there are hopes and passions inside you, waiting to come alive. You know there is so much more you have to offer, though you don't say it out loud. You've carried these dreams in your heart for too long, it's now time—way past time—to do something about them. Life is not a stationary experience. Your dreams are not a portrait fixed in time but a story still being written. Even if all your dreams have come true, there is never a time to stop dreaming. When you stop dreaming, you stop living.

To live our lives fully, we must not only dream and discover, but we must also be ready and willing to continually adapt. If dreaming is about imagining a future worth pursuing, and exploring is about curiosity and continuous learning, then the next critical attribute for living at our highest level is choosing to adapt—to continually reinvent ourselves.

EXTREME MAKEOVER

Very few of us know at an early age what we're going to be when we grow up. Even fewer actually fulfill our dreams about what we want to become or what we want to do. It's a lot to expect an eight-year-old to accurately assess his or her gifts, talent, intelligence, skills, passions, experiences, and career options.

When it comes to the future,

our lives are more discovered

than determined.

It's the same with our relationship with God. There is rarely writing on the wall or a voice in the night. For most of us, walking with God is a mysterious journey of faith and discovery. I wish that the moment we entered a relationship with Jesus, God would send us a memo that spelled out everything. *Erwin, this is what you need to do and give your life to. Here is what you're going to be really good at, and attached is the paint-by-numbers version of how to create the life of your dreams.*

Life is not a color-within-the-lines project;

life is a work of art.

You have to keep mixing colors,

creating new blends,

and seeing things in fresh ways.

You must be willing

to get paint

all over you.

Life is about growth. Growth

demands change. Change

requires humility.

Sometimes you need to bring change;

sometimes you need to *be* changed.

When outside pressures try to pull you down, you must resist them and instead pull everyone else up. Sometimes only the stubborn bring the change the world needs. This is about refusing to settle for the status quo. We should not confuse this with a refusal to adapt and be, as Gandhi described, the change we want to see in the world. You may be so set in your ways, so patterned and regimented, that you hide behind your convictions and beliefs to cloak your fear of change. The Scriptures tell us that God "is the same yesterday, today, and forever" (Heb. 13:8); yet he was willing to become a human for our sake. You can't model your life after Jesus and be unwilling to adapt.

Even when you have an intimate relationship with God, you might find yourself heading full steam ahead in the wrong direction. Or it may be that your life is suddenly making a sharp left turn. You find yourself in a crisis and feel as if you've given yourself to the wrong dream all along.

One afternoon, my wife Kim had one of those dramatic moments where the emotions are greater than the problem. She interrupted my peace by calling frantically, "Erwin come here, come here!" I thought, *What in the world is happening?* She was in the back room watching one of her favorite shows, *Monarch of the Glen*, on BBC. It is a little too slow for me, but Kim is a huge *Monarch of the Glen* fan.

She had been distraught and disappointed because the show had gotten rid of most of the characters she had grown to love over the seasons. She grumbled that the show was ruined. She had complained all the way through the season (while never missing an episode) until this night, when she said enthusiastically,

"They've reinvented it with new characters and new stories. It's wonderful!"

Many of us need reinvented lives. We are living a rerun, and we need fresh stories, maybe some new characters to enter our story. When you get up in the morning, maybe you feel that your life is just a show waiting to be canceled, an endless rerun with worn-out story lines and superficial characters.

If you're going to engage in a journey with God, if you are going to follow the God who created you, if you're going to explore mysterious, dangerous, unknown, uncertain places—then you need to know how to reinvent yourself. You have to learn how to adapt.

When you read some of the stories in the Old Testament, you learn something not just about God's activity in human history, but about how God works through different kinds of cultures and different kinds of people. One of the amazing things about the Jewish people is that under incredible oppression, under extraordinary difficulty, time and time again in different environments and circumstances (almost always oppressive), they have managed not only to survive but also to thrive. They have found ways in the midst of persecution to accomplish extraordinary things that have guided and shaped the course of human history.

Two of those individuals are known simply as Daniel and Esther. In this chapter, we will observe their stories to see how they learned how to adapt, to reinvent themselves, to reshape and reform themselves to face whatever crisis or challenge was in front of them. Because if you're going to dare to imagine and pursue the dreams God has for your life, if you're going to create the life of your dreams you have to be willing and ready to change.

The skills and competencies and experiences you've had in the past will not be enough for every challenge you will face in the future. They are enough to prepare you, but not enough to sustain you. You must build on the past but live for the future.

Daniel and Esther both had the ability to adapt. Both of their stories are set in crisis. Neither had an ideal situation; their circumstances were leveraged for them to fail rather than succeed. All too often we allow ourselves to believe that people who accomplish great things somehow stumble on opportunity or gain an unfair advantage over the rest of us. Yet we find that most often quite the opposite is true. Let's look at how it all began for Daniel.

In the third year of the reign of Jehoiakim king of Judah, Nebuchadnezzar king of Babylon came to Jerusalem and besieged it [attacked and conquered it]. And the Lord delivered Jehoiakim king of Judah into his hand, along with some of the articles from the temple of God. These he carried off to the temple of his god in Babylonia and put in the treasure house of his god.

Then the king ordered Ashpenaz, chief of his court officials, to bring into the king's service some of the Israelites from the royal family and the nobility.

This is what's going on: Israel has been conquered again. They have experienced throughout history conquest, domination, slavery, and oppression. Whether under the Egyptians, Babylonians, Persians, or Romans, the Israelites are forced to continuously explore what it means to be a follower of the living God under the worst of conditions. When this story of Daniel takes place, the Israelites are Babylonian captives with Nebuchadnezzar, the opposing, controlling, conquering king. He takes for himself foreign men as slaves so that they can advance his purpose. The Babylonians also take the articles from the temple of the living God and move them into a temple for pagan gods. In the middle of this crisis, Daniel is brought to Babylon as a slave. Not a good start for a great life.

Esther's story is similar.

> Now there was in the citadel of Susa a Jew of the tribe of Benjamin, named Mordecai . . . who had been carried into exile from Jerusalem by Nebuchadnezzar king of Babylon, among those taken captive with Jehoiachin king of Judah. Mordecai had a cousin named Hadassah, whom he had brought up because she had neither father nor mother. This young woman, who was also known as Esther, had a lovely figure and was beautiful. Mordecai had taken her as his own daughter when her father and mother died.
>
> When the king's order and edict had been proclaimed, many young women were brought to the citadel of Susa and put under the care of Hegai. Esther also was taken to the king's palace and entrusted to Hegai, who had charge of the harem.

Now before you try to romanticize this story, let's consider what's going on. Israel is again captive to a foreign empire. This time it's King Xerxes of the Medes and the Persians controlling the destiny, or so it seems, of the Israelites. King Xerxes gets irritated with the queen and looks for a new wife. He holds a beauty contest, and among the beautiful women selected is a young woman named Esther—a Jewish virgin who has been ripped away from the only family she had left. Her future has been reduced to becoming a glorified prostitute for a man she cannot stomach, much less love. The king sees Esther among his harem and decides he wants her. This is not *Cinderella*. This is not a Harlequin romance novel. This is not a love story, at least not yet. Esther is taken as a slave and put in the harem of King Xerxes. He is a king who sees himself as a god. To the king, Esther is his possession, and she is in the palace for nothing more than his pleasure and to do his bidding.

There's nothing romantic, poetic, or beautiful about this story so far. Before Esther was taken as a slave, she was an orphan. Her mother and father had been killed, so her uncle Mordecai had raised her. As if there wasn't already enough tragedy in her life to turn her heart and soul against God, now this happens.

The stories of Daniel and Esther remind us that we do not get to choose the context from where we begin our story, where our lives begin.

You don't get to choose your parents,
>your race, or your skin color;
you don't get to choose
>your language or economic condition
>>when you're born into this world.
You don't get any say about the beginning
>of your life journey,
>>but you have a great deal
>>>to say about
>the destination of your journey
>>and how that journey shapes you.

LIQUID METAL

Your circumstances do not determine your opportunities. Or if they do, it may well be quite the opposite than you expect. The more challenging your circumstances, the greater your opportunity to see God raise you to new levels of living. When life is overwhelming, it provides the context for you to experience something truly breathtaking. After all, if the world were flat, there would be no mountains to climb.

Some of us live in a context of comfort, and it has become easy for us to settle for safe rather than to disturb the status quo. If you are living a life you don't want to live, the great danger is to accept boredom and monotony as normal. If you're not living the life of your dreams, if you wake up with that little bit of sadness in the mornings because you know you're underachieving, living a life of mediocrity, and choosing average, it's easy to blame everyone else for your condition. Especially when your condition is really good, but not the dream God has for you. You're not called to settle for the good life; you are called to a life of greatness.

Now, there are people in this world who are born into such desperate conditions that their opportunities are dramatically limited. There are people born in the midst of famines, starvation, and unimaginable hardship. They live in a crisis, an epidemic, a pandemic. There are people who are born in lands where there is no water, no food, no freedom. Anyone who says that every follower of Jesus Christ is going to have health and wealth is terribly mistaken (or brain-dead). There are a lot of wonderful, faithful, and faith-filled people whose greatest challenge is survival. They are the true models of courage. Sadly, for many survival is their heroic act. Ironically, many of them are more passionate about life than those of us who have unparalleled privilege and opportunity.

It may be that your challenge is to not allow your context to justify your underachievement. It's an easy thing to do, isn't it? You can look at someone who has a better life, better circumstances, and more opportunities, and say, "Well, the reason I'm not living the life of my dreams is I didn't get all the advantages that he has or she has." I recently heard someone whining because of the incredible oppression they were experiencing as a graduate student at Princeton. I thought, *You are the cultural elite with the backdrop of an entire planet that couldn't even imagine the opportunity you have and you're complaining!*

Your circumstances do not equal your opportunity, because your opportunity is shaped not simply by your external factors but by the internal factors of who you choose to be and become. It would have been so easy for Daniel to say, "I am a slave. I've just been ripped out of the life I love, and now I have to give my life to this King Nebuchadnezzar, this pagan king. I'm supposed to somehow advance his cause." You could justify for Daniel a decision to move to a life of apathy and indifference.

If you were Esther, you would experience the trauma of losing your parents, growing up as an orphan, then being ripped away from the only family you know to become a slave in the harem of a pagan king. In those circumstances, what kind of choices would you begin to make? Would you use that as your reason for underachieving, your excuse to stop adapting and achieving?

But Daniel and Esther did not allow their circumstances to limit their opportunity. We do not get the luxury of choosing the time or the place we were born; nor do we always have control over the circumstances into which we are sometimes thrown. Have you taken personal responsibility for the opportunities given to you? The reason we need to adapt is because we don't get to choose the starting point. Unless you learn how to adapt to your environment, to your circumstances, and to your challenges, you will continue to use them as an excuse, claiming they are the obstacles that stop you from living the life of your dreams.

As the story continues, we find that both Daniel and Esther

learned how to adapt in very difficult contexts where they were slaves, lived under oppression, and had every excuse for not accomplishing anything significant. But instead of accepting their fate and drifting into obscurity, they stepped up, learned everything they could using all they had (even against overwhelming odds), and rose above their circumstances. It was in the context of unimaginable difficulty that they were formed into extraordinary individuals.

Let's go back to Daniel.

> Then the king ordered Ashpenaz, chief of his court officials, to bring into the king's service some of the Israelites from the royal family and the nobility [individuals of incredible wealth and power in their own culture]—young men without any physical defect, handsome, showing aptitude for every kind of learning, well informed, quick to understand, and qualified to serve in the king's palace. He was to teach them the language and literature of the Babylonians. The king assigned them a daily amount of food and wine from the king's table. They were to be trained for three years, and after that they were to enter the king's service.

We are back to step two in our process of living wide awake— explore. Those who were motivated to learn and allowed themselves to continue to grow rose to the top. It would have been easy to confuse a refusal to change as a stand against corruption. There are times when the greatest act of courage and the best evidence of character is the willingness to change. This was one of those moments. Daniel came to Babylon in the worst of circumstances. He overcame the challenges he was forced to face by adapting to them. He was fueled by an insatiable curiosity and determination to learn whatever he needed to thrive in this hostile environment.

He would soon find in his circumstances an incredible opportunity to develop and grow. While once considered an expert, now Daniel's Jewish education was considered obsolete; he would have to retool himself if he was to survive, much less distinguish himself among the young men in the palace. What stayed with him were the competencies that had distinguished him in the past. What he had learned wasn't as important as that he was a learner. Now he would pass the next step in his test—his journey to greatness. Could he adapt?

Here, Daniel's willingness and ability to adapt would be stretched to its limits. He would have to learn the wisdom and ways of the Babylonians, even though they conflicted with his own. He not only did so, but he excelled even above the Babylonians themselves. He had surpassed his captors in achievement and understanding. He simply became the best.

If we are to live our destiny, we must be willing and ready to face the same challenge. All of us must choose to reinvent ourselves to face whatever is waiting in front of us. Part of learning to reinvent yourself is learning how to be teachable, resourceful, and flexible.

While we don't have any control over the way people judge our appearance, Daniel and Esther were young and without any physical defect, we are told. Well, I'm not that young anymore, and I have all kinds of physical defects, so we'll just move past this one. Now it doesn't hurt them any that Daniel is described as handsome and Esther as beautiful. Still there are some things that we can do something about: "showing aptitude for every kind of learning, well informed, quick to understand, and qualified to serve in the king's palace."

What the Bible tells us about Daniel, Meshach, Shadrach, and

Abednego—and also about Esther —is that they were quick studies. They were learners who did not allow their adverse circumstances to limit their potential. They left no room for excuses. They assessed their circumstances, adapted to their environment, and rose to the challenge. Though they were at a deficit, they emerged as the elite. Their lives would be seen as a tragedy if they had not risen up to greatness. Later we are told that Daniel's three friends were thrown into a fiery furnace and survived. Everyone who follows the course to which God has called them will have their mettle tested and will become moldable metal.

Esther was placed under the care of a man named Hegai, who was in charge of the harem. Hegai soon comes to love Esther. He has so much regard for her that he begins to give her insight on how to win the king's heart. So instead of resisting his counsel, Esther learned everything she could from Hegai and literally learned how to become the queen. Both Daniel and Esther were more than a pretty face. They had substance behind the shell.

RAISING THE BAR

When you face challenges and obstacles, you have to learn how to either overcome them or adapt to them. Wisdom guides you to the best choice. To adapt is not to surrender but to become unstoppable. It is the difference between being a boulder or a river. Many of us see virtue as being immovable.

Yet in times of crisis, it is our willingness to be adaptable that distinguishes us.

Conviction is a popular excuse for rigidity, but faith should actually make us more pliable, not less.

What we find in all these individuals through whom God has written biblical history is that faith gives you the confidence to adapt to your circumstance while never compromising your convictions.

You either adapt when you face circumstances you cannot control, or you allow them to become the boundaries of your life. They will establish the parameters of your freedom, define your limits, and diminish your dreams—and that is where you stop. I may not know anything about you or your life journey, but I know this. You can't control the context from which your life story is being written, but you can control the content.

Life is filled with unforeseen boulders, and you must become the river. The higher the water, the less the boulders can slow its progress. A great destiny is not a tightrope but a river. It is not balance you need but adaptability. Missteps are permissible but not rigidity. You must be willing to reimagine, to relearn, and to reinvent yourself.

Adaptability requires teachability. The ability to change comes from one core characteristic, and that is simply *humility*. Humility keeps us flexible. It serves as an oil that keeps our hearts open to change and able to adjust.

I am astonished by how many people use their faith as an excuse to remain in ignorance. It sounds so spiritual. "All I need to know is the Bible." Really? Is that really what God says? Is this what the Scriptures teach? Is that the model we find throughout biblical history? Is this really the way of Jesus?

Isn't it strange how it says of these heroes of old that these young men were characterized for having "aptitude for every kind of learning"? They are described as "well informed, quick to understand, and qualified to serve in the king's palace." Also we find that they were required to learn the language and literature of the Babylonians. They had to learn how to be Babylonians, how to thrive in a Babylonian world, and they had to learn an entirely new language and entirely new worldview and an entirely new way of thinking. And yet the Bible goes on to tell us that they were extraordinary:

> To these four young men God gave knowledge and understanding of all kinds of literature and learning. And Daniel could understand visions and dreams of all kinds. . . . In every matter of wisdom and understanding about which the king questioned them, he found them ten times better than all the magicians and enchanters in his whole kingdom.

If you are a sincere follower of Christ, then you are mandated by God to be a voracious, intentional learner. You cannot allow yourself to settle, to be less than your best in whatever field or endeavor you have committed yourself to. You must always strive toward excellence in whatever you pursue. And you are not allowed to ignore the world around you—otherwise known as the real world! You are not supposed to be a relic of the past or even a preserver of the past. You are to be in the world making it a better place to live. Rise to the top and see what God can do with your life. This doesn't always mean you will be the best in the world at what you do, but you are supposed to be the world's best you.

Bring your best and move forward with confidence that God's incredible ingenuity will use even your shortcomings to do amazing things through your life. I love this about Daniel and Esther—they did what they could and let God fill in the blanks where they didn't know how it could possibly work out. They let God fill in the gap when their abilities and intelligence were simply not enough.

An Endless Resource

Now Esther's challenge was a little different than Daniel's. Her story is unusual. Basically, she is thrown into a beauty pageant—one she doesn't want to be in. When the king's order was given and his edict proclaimed, many of the young women were brought to be cared for by Hegai. The book of Esther says that Esther pleased Hegai, and he provided her with beauty treatments and special food (Est. 2:9). Before a young woman's turn came to go in to King Xerxes, she had to complete twelve months of beauty treatments prescribed for the women, six months with oil of myrrh and six with perfumes and cosmetics.

I was astonished when I heard that Ryan Seacrest of *American Idol* spends six hours getting ready for his show. *Six hours.* But can you imagine spending twelve months getting ready for one date? A lot of us would still be single if that were the standard we had to live up to.

Esther's story explains:

And this is how she would go to the king: Anything she wanted was given to her to take with her from the harem to the king's palace. In the evening she would go there and in the morning return to another part of the harem to the care of Shaashgaz, the king's eunuch who was in charge of the concubines. She would not return to the king unless he was pleased with her and summoned her by name.

When the turn came for Esther (the young woman Mordecai had adopted, the daughter of his uncle Abihail) to go to the king, she asked for nothing other than what Hegai, the king's eunuch who was in charge of the harem, suggested. And Esther won the favor of everyone who saw her.

Esther learned how to work the system. If you're going to continue to reinvent yourself and allow nothing to stop you from fulfilling the destiny God created you to accomplish, you must be humble enough to remain teachable and teachable enough to remain adaptable. You have to learn from anyone and everyone in any and every context. You have to have an open mind and an open heart and recognize that in every discipline and every field, there is something you can learn that will help you become a better person and advance God's purpose for your life.

But you also need to be resourceful. The word *resource* is not one of those instantaneously compelling words. Actually it's a really boring word. It just means stuff, supply, things, materials. Not that exciting, right?

But the word *resourceful* is a very exciting word. When you look at the word *resourceful*, it means ingenious, creative, imaginative, quick-witted. What happened between *resource* and *resourceful*? I think it's that "full" part. When you stop at *resource*, you're at best a human container of gifts and talents and intellect, passions and abilities, but you do nothing with that resource; essentially, you are boring. You're just stuff, means, supply, or material. But when you become resourceful and start pulling out the stuff God has placed inside of you and start drawing on that creativity, intellect, talent, and experience that God stored within you and start becoming resourceful, then you become extraordinary and begin to develop your own uniqueness.

Daniel and Esther were so teachable, they learned from their captors. They learned from Babylonians and Persians. They learned from everyone who was willing to teach them. But they were also resourceful. They did not underestimate the gifts and talents and capacity God had placed within their very being.

Daniel and Esther were flexible. Another good word—*flexible* means to bend without breaking. As a follower of Jesus Christ, you need to learn how to be flexible. You need to learn how to bend without breaking. Often people of faith are perceived as dogmatic, rigid, and unchanging. Do you know why? Well, because they are dogmatic, rigid, and unchanging. The perception is pretty accurate.

Part of the dilemma of believing in God is that you can actually begin to act like you are God. You're always right, never wrong. The way you do everything is the way everyone should do it. Many of us end up being convinced that when anybody does something different than we do it, says something differently than we do, when anyone approaches life in any way different than we do, then that person is absolutely in the wrong. And we are convinced that our perspective and God's perspective are exactly the same thing.

Ironically, this happens not when you have more faith but less faith.

We become dogmatic as a result of fear,
        not faith.
    Faith keeps you flexible and postured
            for change.
        Faith ignites courage, not
                conformity.
    Fear seeks to control; faith seeks
            to create.

This doesn't mean you don't have convictions but that you understand what your nonnegotiables are. Some things are your core; everything else can change.

ESSENTIAL KNOWLEDGE

To be adaptable, you have to know what's important, what's essential. Improvisation is not the result of shooting from the hip but knowing where you're aiming.

> Spontaneity is rapid action
> in response to unforeseen circumstances
> informed by previously determined
> values.

You can respond faster when you have decided ahead of time. You are more adaptable when you have clarity about who you are and why you are here.

I was on my way to a meeting with our former high school student leader. He had asked me to help him bring together his core team for their organizational leadership meeting. He felt the meeting's success was critical for their future as a team. Like in many organizations, just because you work together, that doesn't make you a team. Although this group of leaders had been working together for quite some time, he was having a difficult time helping them come together as an effective and cohesive team. He was intense and passionate, and his team reflected his temperament and was extremely loyal to his leadership.

As we were driving there, I asked him what I thought was an easy question: "Before we get there, could you tell me what your core values are so that I don't violate them inadvertently?" I didn't want to go in and superimpose my values, say some things with the wrong assumptions, and end up doing more harm than good. I could really mess things up for him. I said, "Tell me what your nonnegotiables are, and I promise I will not challenge them publicly. This is your team; I'm just here to listen and help you."

He got really quiet, and I thought maybe he didn't want to tell me or didn't trust me. I wasn't sure. But then again, he asked me to go with him, so he trusted me, right?

So I pressed further. "Really, whatever they are, just tell me. No judgment." And he wouldn't make eye contact, and I could not figure out what in the world was going on.

Finally he said, "I have no idea what my nonnegotiables are."

I knew in that moment why he was so rigid and controlling as a leader. I responded, "This is why you're so dogmatic. If you don't know what your nonnegotiables are, you won't negotiate anything. You're afraid to let go of anything because later you might discover that was a nonnegotiable. When you don't know what's really important, you treat everything the same. Adaptability is not the result of a hollow core, but of clarity and conviction about what is at your core. Don't confuse being rigid and unchanging with having convictions."

Some of us are more like coconuts—hard on the outside and hollow in the center. But we need to be more like peaches—soft and fuzzy on the outside but solid as a rock in the middle. This dramatically changes the way others experience us as well as how we will experience life.

Daniel and Esther knew there was a difference between what it means to adopt and what it means to adapt. One is to surrender to overwhelming circumstances; the other is to rise above them. To adopt is to compromise your convictions; to adapt is to live them out in the real world.

CORE TRAINING

This leads me to another unacceptable option—to abdicate. Too often we have called our detachment from the world around us an expression of holiness when in truth it is an abdication of our responsibility to serve humanity and make the world a better place.

At the beginning of Daniel's story, we are told, "Among those who were chosen were some from Judah: Daniel, Hananiah, Mishael and Azariah. The chief official gave them new names: to Daniel, the name Belteshazzar; to Hananiah, Shadrach; to Mishael, Meshach; and to Azariah, Abednego."

So here they are, slaves of a foreign king. They've lost everything they treasure, and if that were not bad enough, they were now going to lose their identities. Their Jewish names not only were a statement of their culture but actually a declaration of their God. Their names were a promise and a vow that their lives belong to the living God—the one true God. But now under the authority of Nebuchadnezzar, these young men are renamed. Instead of having names that honor God, they are given Babylonian names that honor the king and his pagan gods. I can assure you, throughout your life there will be people who want to tell you who you are and try to define who you should become. And you are going to have to struggle through what it means to adapt but not adopt. But the struggle is worth it. You must never run from the challenge an simply abdicate responsibility.

Daniel was renamed, but it just didn't stick. I think, in part, it was a result of the power of his self-identity. He knew who he was; no one was going to define him. He would not abdicate, he would not adopt. But watch him adapt. He resolved not to defile himself with the royal food and wine. He asked the chief official for permission not to dishonor his God and to be exempt from participating in something that would violate his faith.

> Now God had caused the official to show favor and compassion to Daniel, but the official told Daniel, "I am afraid of my lord the king, who has assigned your food and drink. Why should he see you looking worse than the other young men your age? The king would then have my head because of you."
>
> Daniel then said to the guard whom the chief official had appointed over Daniel, Hanaiah, Mishael and Azariah, "Please test your servants for ten days: Give us nothing but vegetables to eat and water to drink. Then compare our appearance with that of the young men who eat the royal food, and treat your servants in accordance with what you see." So he agreed to this and tested them for ten days.
>
> At the end of the ten days they looked healthier and better nourished than any of the young men who ate the royal food. So the guard took away their choice food and the wine they were to drink and gave them vegetables instead.

First of all, since I live in LA, I need to emphasize that this is not a passage saying we should all be vegans. It's not a passage saying drinking wine is wrong. You may be more inclined toward one than the other. This is a test of character, not diet. Daniel was being offered the king's choice food and drink. He understood that if he ate the food and drank the wine, it would be a declaration that he was now worshiping the king of Babylon and the gods of the Babylonians.

Now here's the strange thing (and the point). When Daniel and his friends were given Babylonian names, they didn't protest. They took on their new names. In fact, Daniel's companions are better known by their Babylonian names than they are by their Hebrew names. They are known as Meshach, Shadrach, and Abednego—and history has made their names as famous a trio as Moe, Curly, and Larry. They were willing to embrace the changes that came in this new climate, but they would not allow themselves to change their core.

What is at your core? Do you have any convictions for which you would be willing to risk everything? Are there any convictions you would not give up under the pressure cooker of life?

More than ten years ago, I was playing basketball with a friend, and I landed flat-footed and jarred my back out of place. I had never had back problems, and it was painful. I did everything I knew how to do. I went to a doctor who treated Joe Montana, and he put hypodermic needles in my back and shot cortisone into it. I never went back. I realized they were just numbing Joe and throwing him back in the game. I didn't want to go in the game; I wanted to live. I went to a physical therapist, and still nothing helped. I knew nothing about chiropractors and put them in the same category as acupuncture. I hate needles and was terrified of what a chiropractor might do to me. I went to everybody I thought might offer me some relief. I couldn't stand up straight for almost a year.

I had finally become desperate enough to be open to a nontraditional approach when a chiropractor came to me and asked if he could help. It's pretty obvious and embarrassing when you're speaking at an angle. I remember going to one particular physical therapist, and he started digging into my stomach, which aside from being really awkward was painful. And I said, "What are you doing? It's my back. You've got the wrong side." He explained calmly that everything is connected to your abdomen. Everything is in some way held together by your stomach, and you have to work on the stomach to help you with your back.

He introduced me to the physiological concept of what is called your core. And what is really trendy right now is core training. The history of core training comes from various cultures, but the backstory in the States comes from when POWs were being killed because they looked too strong and therefore were more likely to be high risk. The POWs who looked anemic and weak were allowed to live. So if they exercised, they were risking their lives. But they didn't want to get so weak that if an opportunity to escape availed itself, they could not take it. So they began working on their core, strengthening their center even though they looked weak on the outside.

I think a lot of us choose the opposite path. We do the tanning booth and the Botox and the collagen so we can look healthy on the outside, but we're really weak in our center.

If you want to reinvent yourself, you have to know who you are and who you long to be and not violate that on the journey. At the same time, you must strengthen your core in order to be flexible in every other area of your life.

THE POWER TO CHANGE

The *Harvard Business Review* published an article by David Roak and William Torburg entitled "The Seven Transformations of Leadership." It proposes that leaders are made, not born, and how they develop is critical for organizational change. The authors suggest that leadership is more about what they call *action logic*. Most developmental psychologists agree that what differentiates leaders is not so much their philosophy of leadership, their personality, or even their style of management; rather, it's their internal action logic, how they interpret their surroundings or react when their power or safety has been challenged.

Roak and Torburg give us seven different ways of leading, seven different action logics. They describe the seven approaches: the opportunist, the diplomat, the expert, the achiever, the individualist, the strategist, and then their ultimate approach toward leadership, the alchemist. I'm not going to break them down here; I just want to highlight their highest level, the alchemist. We are told, "The final leadership action logic for which we have data and experience is the alchemist. Our studies of the few leaders we have identified as alchemists suggests that what sets them apart from strategists, which is the next level of leadership, is their ability to renew or even reinvent themselves and their organizations in historically significant ways." By the way, the unique achievement of alchemists is that they generate social transformation by integrating material, spiritual, and societal transformation. I am convinced all of us can change and each of us can bring change. For too long we have focused exclusively on being good rather than doing good. Transformation is at the core of our faith. We are called by God to renew our minds for the promise of transformation. In this sense we are all alchemists; or at least we all have the potential to ignite social transformation. When you awaken the hero within you, you find not only the artist and the explorer but also the alchemist. It is not enough to simply be good; we must also do good.

Even the business world understands we human beings have the capacity to change, the ability to reinvent ourselves, and the potential to adapt and improve. But if nothing so far motivates you to embrace a value for personal and continuous change, let me give you one more reason: learning to adapt is essential to creating the life of your dreams.

And this isn't just about you and your life. You cannot help others change unless you are willing to change. The world desperately needs the power of your life fully lived. You have no greater responsibility than to live the life God created you to live. To live your life at your highest level empowers you to give your life for the greatest good. For you to make your greatest contribution, you must dream, discover, and adapt. You must be willing to change, and the greater your ability to change, the greater your ability to bring change. It is here your journey requires you to be artist, explorer, and alchemist.

From the very beginning, the movement of Jesus has been about change. It is not incidental that the central figure of the first century personified the radical change that would define this new movement. He would change the course of history, but first everything in his life would change.

There may not have been anyone more rigid in the Scriptures than a guy named Saul. Saul later became the apostle Paul. It wasn't just his name that changed. He reinvented himself—or more accurately, God re-created him and then ignited a journey of reinvention. Saul hated Christians. He despised them with a passion. Saul was so certain that Christians were wrong that he set out to have them killed. He was there for the stoning of the first Christian martyr, Stephen, and he actually received permission from the religious leaders of his time to hunt down Christians and either imprison them or have them assassinated.

One day, while traveling down a road named Damascus in Syria, he was confronted with the reality of Jesus Christ. He had a face-to-face encounter with the living God and his life was changed forever.

Later this same Paul would write,

> I am free, I belong to no one. I have made myself a slave to every-
> one to win as many as possible. To the Jews I became like a Jew to
> win the Jews. To those under the law I became like one under the
> law (though I myself am not under the law), so as to win those
> under the law. To those not having the law I became like one not
> having the law (though I am not free from God's law but am
> under Christ's law, so as to win those not having the law). To the
> weak I became weak, to win the weak. I have become all things to
> all people so that by all possible means I might save some. I do all
> this for the sake of the gospel, that I may share in its blessings.

While our dreams may be different, and each of us has a unique
path to walk, this I know is true for you if Jesus Christ guides
your life—your life can never be simply about you. It can't be
only about your goals, your ambitions, your dreams, or your life.
Paul was determined to become whatever he needed to become
to help as many people as possible find the life-transforming
relationship that comes in Jesus Christ. He resolved, "If I need
to be a Jew, I'll be a Jew; if I need to be a Greek, I'll be a Greek; if
I need to be a slave, I'll be a slave; if I need to be free, I'll be free;
if I need to be weak, I'll be weak. I'll become all things to all men
that I might save some." Pay attention to Paul's words, "I become
all things to all men." Paul adapts for the sake of others. For Paul,
Jesus didn't come only to save him, but so that he could join with
Jesus in saving others.

Paul knew what was at his core. No one around Paul would ever
say he was soft or without conviction. No one would ever accuse
Paul of not having a backbone. If anything, Paul was one tough

dude. He was immovable at his core. And his core moved him toward the heart and purpose of God. He was driven to serve the world and to bring the world into relationship with Jesus Christ. At the same time, he learned how to adapt, how to reinvent himself, how to become the kind of person he needed to be without losing who he really was in the midst of his circumstances. Paul changed because who he was at his core changed. Saul became Paul and not only did his name change but everything he cared about. Once his life was fueled by religious arrogance and self-righteousness and now his life was reduced to one motive—love.

In Paulo Coelho's novel *The Alchemist,* he describes young Santiago the central character of his story having a conversation with the wind. The wind reminds him that "everything has its own Personal Legend—each of us has a path that leads to our own destiny and personal greatness." The wind continues, "But you can't turn into the wind." Santiago responds, "Just teach me to be the wind for the a few moments. . . . So you and I can talk about the limitless possibilities of people and the winds."

Santiago, like many of us, wishes he could know such freedom. Yet as adaptable as the wind is, we find it cannot compare to the limitless nature of love. It is those who know love who are the envy of the wind. Speaking of love the boy explains, "When you are loved, you can do anything in creation. When you are loved there's no need at all to understand what's happening, because everything happens within you, and even men can turn themselves into the wind. As long as the wind helps, of course."

To adapt is not always an easy thing. Sometimes it takes all your strength and energy to do so. Often it will take great courage. It is simply easier to stay the same; to refuse to change and insist that the world adapt to you. Too often we see our rigidity as a virtue. Character does not make you hard; nor does it make you soft. Character makes you pliable while never violating your core. In all of this it is love that keeps us more adaptable than the wind.

When you are loved, you no longer fear change nor are you afraid to change. When you love you are willing to embrace the sacrifice of change and make the sacrifices to change. When you live a life of love, you are not bound to who you are but to who you will become. Love transforms. It leaves nothing it touches as it was before its caress. The only thing you need to change is love.

Do you want to create the life of your dreams? Then you have to learn to adapt, because you're going to face challenges and crises and obstacles and barricades; and if you are rigid and un-changing, they will be defined by the boundaries and limits of your life. But if you allow God to make you pliable, liquid, fluid, adaptable, you will discover that God will always work through you in such an amazing way that nothing will stop you from creating the life God wants to breathe into your imagination.

The Scriptures tell us, "If anyone is in Christ, he is a new creation." A metamorphosis takes place. You are forever changed. "The old is gone, the new has come!"

The Bible is all about change. Those words you hear describing what God does in us—they're all a form of change:

Transformation means change.

Conversion means change.

Repentance means change.

Sanctification means (yep, you guessed it) change.

All the words that describe your spiritual journey, what happens to you, they're all about change. And if you're going to be a follower of Christ, get ready for change, because who you are today is not who you will be tomorrow. You are changing. The world is changing. You are a change agent. Allow your dreams to unleash the endless possibilities. Keep fueling your insatiable curiosity. Then look at your circumstances as the crucible from which your dreams will be forged into reality.

Get ready to dream, to discover, and to adapt. This is the beginning of living an awakened life—of living wide awake.

expect 4

THE BELIEVER

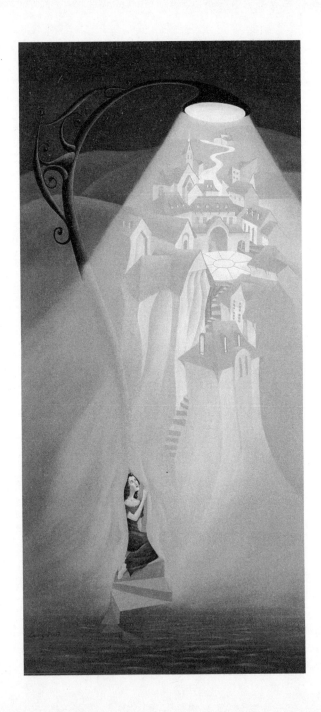

HAVE YOU EVER NOTICED THAT PEOPLE CAN HAVE dramatically different views of the same moment in life? On a recent family trip to Paris, we were greeted with rain on our second day. Kim and Mariah were so happy. They love the rain. I had different feelings about the weather that day. Their enthusiasm was even a little irritating. A week later we were in Rome, and as a gift I had them do the chick thing and get their hair done. A couple of weeks on the road can make you look pretty rough. I patiently waited, wandering the streets near the Pantheon. Kim and Mariah both looked stunning as they stepped out of the salon. It wasn't thirty minutes when the heavens opened and we were drenched walking from cover to cover for almost two hours trying to get back to our hotel. I was having a blast; they were having a bad hair day.

Sometimes our circumstances can change our perceptions and perspectives. Still, there are some people who seem to see everything as a glass half-empty, people who are filled with pessimism, always cynical. They can't seem to embrace, maintain, or reflect optimism. It's as if they have been punctured somewhere deep within their souls. They have a leak when it comes to hope. They seem incapable of holding on to a positive view of life. Then there are others who see the glass as always half-full. They are always filled with enthusiasm, excitement, and hopeful anticipation.

Several years ago one of the forerunners and leaders in the field of positive psychology, Martin Seligman, wrote a book called *Learned*

Optimism. He observed that certain people have an extraordinary ability to overcome difficulties, obstacles, and even failure. The key, it seems, is that how they relate to failure is dramatically different from those who tend to be overwhelmed and paralyzed by their failures. The optimistic never see failure as personal, permanent, or pervasive, but others are constricted, paralyzed, or controlled by failures.

If you're going to create the life of your dreams, you're going to face a lot of failure, difficulty, and obstacles. You're going to be informed by the world around you that you cannot accomplish what you are setting out to do or become the person you long to become. You will be told it is impossible to accomplish the goals you long to achieve, to create the life of your dreams.

One of the most important characteristics of people who achieve the extraordinary is they live a life of expectation—they expect the good to happen; they internalize optimism.

LEANING FORWARD

The book of Hebrews describes some of the early followers of Jesus Christ as they faced extraordinary opposition and seemingly overwhelmingly insurmountable odds. They became a part of a unique tribe that would never shrink back, but always moved forward with endless optimism.

> Remember those earlier days after you had received the light, when you endured in a great conflict full of suffering. Sometimes you were publicly exposed to insult and persecution; at other times you stood side by side with those who were so treated. You suffered along with those in prison and joyfully accepted the

confiscation of your property, because you knew that you yourselves had better and lasting possessions. So do not throw away
your confidence; it will be richly rewarded.

You need to persevere so that when you have done the will of
God, you will receive what he has promised. For,

> "In just a little while,
> he who is coming will come
> and will not delay."

And,

> "But my righteous one will live by faith.
> And I take no pleasure
> in the one who shrinks back."

But we are not of those who shrink back and are destroyed, but of
those who believe and are saved.

The early days of this movement don't sound very promising,
do they? If you had to evaluate the likelihood of this movement
surviving, much less thriving, you would probably conclude that
it would die out within one generation. Its founder crucified, and
its core leadership persecuted, martyred, put to death. What are
the chances that those who identify themselves with Jesus Christ
and call themselves his followers would endure such hardship?

And if you thought it couldn't get any worse, listen to this
description of the early Christians' plight: "Sometimes you were
publicly exposed to insult and persecution; at other times you
stood side by side with those who were so treated. You suffered

along with those in prison and joyfully accepted the confiscation of your property, because you knew that you yourselves had better and lasting possessions."

In spite of all this, somehow they kept believing that tomorrow was going to be better than today, that the future had promise worth living for, that enduring whatever hardship came today was worth it because tomorrow was coming.

In his closing remarks, the writer of Hebrews calls these believers to a life of expectation, telling them, "So do not throw away your confidence." He recognizes the real risk that, because of the hardships they faced, those who had found faith could potentially give up their confidence in the future and begin to live a life beneath their potential, beneath their dreams, beneath their destiny. The promise is if we keep our confidence, "it will be richly rewarded"

Why is it that when you talk faith and spirituality, the word *confidence* seems almost a negative attribute? Somehow we have come to see these in conflict with one another—to have faith is to not need confidence. Even if your confidence is in God, isn't it still confidence? It's almost as if you should lack confidence if you are a truly spiritual person, and certainly you should lack confidence if you're a genuinely humble person.

But here the Scriptures are saying don't throw away your confidence, because it will be richly rewarded. You need to lean forward, believing that what God is doing in your life and through your life cannot be thwarted or stopped. "You need to persevere so that when you have done the will of God, you will receive what he has promised. For, 'In just a little while, he who is coming will come and will not delay.' And, 'But my righteous one will live by faith. And I take no pleasure in the one who shrinks back.'"

Of all the things that may change about you when you connect to God, here is one that should fill you with confidence—if you have lived your life running away, this is not who you are any longer. Where once we ran from problems, failures, hardship, danger, and challenges, we are now among those who thrive in the midst of them. You need to know who you are and to which tribe you belong. Other may run in fear, but you are not of those who shrink back. You recognize that the greatness within you can only emerge if you are willing to face your greatest challenges.

Maybe you didn't know that about yourself. Maybe your life history doesn't reflect this. Maybe all your experience tells you that you are inherently a coward, a failure, and a quitter. But God says, "No, you've misunderstood yourself. You've misjudged yourself. You've underestimated yourself." If you are in a relationship with the God who created you, no matter who you've been or what you've done or how many times you've messed up or failed or quit, you are no longer that person, no longer a part of the tribe that shrinks back.

Chad Becker, who serves on our leadership team at Mosaic, once qualified for the US Olympic ski team. He would be the diametrical opposite of me in skiing. For him, skiing is natural; for me, it's unnatural. I still try and continue to hope one day to learn how to ski. I give it a shot every ten years or so.

I've come to realize what has been my problem. See, when you put on those skis, the mountain is going down and the snow is slick. And the natural tendency when you are going in a certain direction really fast with a lot of trees and a ski lodge awaiting your arrival is to pull back, right? Think about it. If you are going too fast, you want to pull back, but there's nothing to pull back on. All you have are those little sticks, which are essentially worthless. So you're pulling back on your skis, thinking, *Slow down, slow down.*

Now they tell you if you lean back you'll lose control, but you know that's not true. They're lying to you. They just don't want you on the mountain taking up space on their snow another day.

"Lean forward," they tell you with a devious grin. But you know you shouldn't lean forward. Why in the world would you lean forward in the direction you are trying not to go? So you keep leaning back, and they nag, "No, if you want to learn how to ski, you have to bend your knees and lean forward in the direction you are going." But you are certain about this: when you don't want to go in a direction, and you definitely don't want to go there faster, if you lean forward, you're going to lose control and go faster and you're going to get hurt.

So you eventually concede and try it their way. You bend your knees and start going faster and think, *Lean forward, lean forward.* You're leaning.

That's what happens when we begin to dabble in this God thing and maybe invite Jesus Christ to change us and lead us into a new lives. What we really want God to do is be the calming presence in our life. We want God to bring some peace and stability. But soon you're saying, "Wait a minute, nobody told me that a relationship with God is like skiing downhill in the Swiss Alps as a beginner with no lessons!"

Of course, we enjoy the ski lift. The ride is so nice, so scenic, so relaxing. It's when you get off the lift and you make the turn that it hits you: "Wait a minute. Where is the lift down?!" Has this been your experience with God? Your life is a mess, you're overwhelmed, you turn to God, and he picks you up and sets you in the lift. And it is beautiful and breathtaking. Then you get to the top and you turn around, and the journey is bigger and more challenging than you ever imagined.

Now what you have is a beautiful mess. There is life inviting you to engage it, to conquer it, to come at it full speed ahead staring at you from below. You hear a haunting but gentle voice whisper into your soul, *Lean forward; don't shrink back.* To create the life of your dreams, you have to lean forward. You have to expect, to believe, to live a life that could actually be described as a life of faith. You must live a life that presses into the future.

GREAT EXPECTATIONS

I don't know if you've realized it yet, but after you enter into a relationship with God, you're not translated into a different universe. You still live in the same world you were in before you came to God. You still have the same life that overwhelmed you before you came to God. You still have the same marriage that challenged you before you came to God. You're still living in the same skin of the person you didn't like before you came to God. You have the same problems, the same weaknesses, the same circumstances, only now the expectations have changed. You are now supposed to live at an entirely new level. You may not fully realize or recognize that what is changing is actually you. The way God changes your life is by changing you.

You've probably already realized that God does not exempt you from the life you created before you came to him. The whole journey begins from wherever you are to wherever you are going. No shortcuts. Wherever you made your mess, that's where you get to start cleaning it up. You don't get to start at the end. But you have to begin with the end in mind. The only future you will give yourself to is the one you believe can happen. You will only give yourself to create a future you believe in. And you will only see that future if you believe it's coming. This is why you have to live in expectation—to internalize optimism.

Faith was never meant to be primarily a noun. It is a verb that denotes action. What do you expect to become? Whoever you are right now, do you have any expectation within you to become a better person? Do you expect your life, your future, to be different because you are a person of faith? Do you expect the world to be different because of your life? So where does your faith, your expectation, stop? Where do you set the boundaries of your expectation? If you can change one thing—one choice, one action, one attitude, one thought—why can't you change your life? Or create a better future? Or at least leave a dent?

Not long ago, I was talking with a businessman about how the expectation of change can be lost when we fail to change. We were having a casual conversation when he asked me what I did for a living. I shared with him that I write books. He went on to ask me what kind. I started sharing about some of the different topics, hoping to find something of interest to him. It was when I started talking about *Uprising* that something caught his attention. I had explained that it was about character transformation, and he said, "What's that?" It might surprise you, but people who aren't in the context of spiritual conversation don't often use the word *transformation*. While organizational change is a common topic, this wasn't an assessable concept. I thought, *How do I explain character transformation to this businessman in one sentence?*

"Transformation is the ability to get up in the morning and look in the mirror and like the person you are becoming," I explained. He looked off into the distance for a moment, looked back my way, and then said, "I would like to get that book."

Sometimes we stop believing we can change. That our lives can change. That the world can change.

Who are you expecting to become? Have you just given up and

settled for saying, "Well, I am who I am." What are you expecting to accomplish with your life? Are you engaging the level of challenge and opportunity that you thought you would or did you have to bring your dreams down to match your life? Have you given up on accomplishing something meaningful and significant? Have you hit a wall? You face problems you can't seem to get past. All those fears, failures, phobias, habits, and addictions hold you captive. You've just accepted where you are as your highest level of living or achievement. You've set in your mind that you'll never get beyond this. You're haunted by the thought, *This is the limit of the life I should expect.*

Failure can become

a state of being, as can

despair.

A life of faith is a life of expectation. The book of Hebrews gives us snapshots of individuals who lived a life of expectation, internalized optimism, and refused to give up. We are called to emulate the lives of women and men who kept leaning into their future. Through their stories, we are given clues about how we can begin to expect more and live bigger than ourselves. We are given this backstory to their epic tales:

Now faith is being sure of what we hope for and certain of what we do not see. This is what the ancients were commended for.

By faith we understand that the universe was formed at God's command, so that what was seen was not made out of what was visible.

Here we find the secret of dreaming with your eyes open. At the core of their ancient faith, their primal faith, these men and women could see the invisible. What drove those who are commended for their faith, what was at the core of those ancients who walked with God, is that they could see that to which most of us remain blind.

"Faith is being sure of what we hope for and certain of what we do not see." A life of expectation is the result of living in the dynamic tension that exists between faith and hope. When you begin to live a life that integrates faith and hope, you begin to internalize optimism. Faith, we are told, is the substance of things hoped for. There is an interconnection between faith and hope.

We find that faith is different from what we've oftentimes thought. Faith isn't so much about having a big idea. Faith isn't about how much belief you can muster up. Faith isn't like spiritual childbirth, where you experience the pain of labor. It is not abut trying to create the future by believing it will be so. Faith is not the Christian version of a wish. It is not about speaking something into reality. Faith is different. Faith is about substance. It's about knowing what has not happened will certainly happen. Not because you will make it happen but because God has promised it will be so. It's a conviction about things unseen. It is the promise of a better world, a better future—a better you.

Faith is about conviction, while hope is about confidence. Faith grounds us in the certainty of God's faithfulness, and hope pulls us into the mystery of God's future.

MUSE OR SIMPLY AMUSING?

Some of us have misunderstood faith. We think we are full of faith when we come to God with great ideas about what he should do and what we could do for him. Often when we hear about faith, it seems like something we have to work up. You can hear your spiritual life coach yelling, "You've got to believe!" You have to believe more; you have to believe God; you have to believe bigger. That's what "faith" is supposedly all about.

The problem with your life, you are told, is you don't have enough faith. The reason you're not rich is you don't have enough faith. The reason you are not healed is you don't have enough faith. The reason you haven't lost that weight is, that's right, not enough faith.

People talk about faith as if it's a magical ingredient that impresses God and gives him a great idea of what he should do with our life. But when you read the consummate chapter on faith in Scripture, it's not like that at all. In fact, not a single person in the eleventh chapter of Hebrews is commended for coming up with the idea.

Let's take Noah. It's not as if God was up in heaven saying, "I created humanity and it's a mess down there. Everything is going wrong. They're destroying everything. Just look at the ozone. It's all going in the wrong direction."

Then Noah stepped up and said, "God, look, the world is in terrible shape. You've really let things get out of hand. Everybody is living decadent and corrupt lives and they're leaving their beer cans in my front yard. God, you need to do something about this!"

And God was like, "I know, I know. It's not at all what I expected. I'm just at a loss for what to do."

So Noah bailed God out: "Look, you were really great with the creative process, but you're a terrible manager. This is what you need to do. See this liquid stuff? You have really underestimated its potential. You have it all locked up in the clouds, stored in the ocean, or coming out of streams. I think you should just let it pour. Call it 'rain.' And what you should do, God, is flood the whole earth. But timing is important. First, I should build an ark. I'll build this big giant boat, and I'll call two of all the animals of the earth so you don't have to re-create them all over again. No need for redundancy. I'm looking out for you, God. And maybe you can flood the earth and start over again with . . . me."

God was so relieved. "Noah, see, this is why I like you. You are inventive, creative; you're a problem solver. Thank you, Noah."

A lot of us think that faith is about impressing God with our ideas or coming up with these huge plans.

It's not as if Moses' life was the result of a pre–burning bush conversation that went something like this: "God, this is ridiculous. We're slaves to Egypt. By the way, why did you send us here? Didn't you foresee that the Egyptians were going to turn on us? I'm not blaming you for all of this, God, but something has to happen, okay? I think what you should do first of all is show up in a bush. That way, I can give you all the credit. And then you send me to Egypt, and I'll speak softly and carry a big stick. No, check that, I'll take a staff. I'll beat them with a stick. Then this is where you come in. You call forth ten plagues. We'll hit them with boils and frogs, nothing really huge at first. Then I'll say, 'Let my people go' and Pharaoh won't at first, but when we really put on the heat he will let us all go free.

And God was like, "Moses I have been sitting here asking myself, *What am I going to do?* For generations I've been waiting for someone who could dream big and get me motivated. Thank you so much."

Then all the people of Israel went free, and God said go right, but the right way was left and they were trapped at the Red Sea. So now the Egyptians were coming and you could almost hear God moaning, "Oh, no. I knew I should have gotten directions." (That's how you know God's a male, right?) And there they were, at a dead-end street, and Moses said to God, "Look, I'll do the hard part; I'll raise the staff. You do the easy part. You part the water. Then we'll just cross right through."

God isn't lacking in vision. But there does seem to be a shortage of people willing to dream as big as God. Faith isn't about convincing God to go big but posturing ourselves to join God in a life bigger than we are and bigger than our dreams. People walk with God, and they are brought into what God is doing and even what he is dreaming. They believe God and connect to his intention in human history.

Faith is about confidence in God's character, that he is good and true and beautiful. There are many things that are uncertain to us, but we know that God is good, that he can be trusted with our lives, and that we should live our lives in pursuit of the future he paints for us—a picture of a better world he promised would come to pass if we would live as if it were our destiny.

PROPELLED BY PROGRESS

Faith is about conviction; hope is about confidence. Hope is what pulls you forward into the future, knowing no matter how bad things get, when you are pursuing the life God created you to live and the future he calls you to create, nothing and no one can stop you. If nothing can stop God, then who can stop you when you are pursuing him and living for his purpose?

Every once in a while I go to a gym and try to exercise. I go at least twelve times a year—a good, biblical number. So I'm there at least once a month. Eventually I found the elliptical machines. They are good when you get older because they are not as hard on your joints, and you feel like you're making progress and really moving. It's a lot of activity, but no forward motion, which could be a metaphor for a lot of my life.

So I'm on the elliptical machine, moving, working, and sweating.

Eventually I start venturing into the different programs—*Choose your terrain*, it instructs me. Wow, all this and air-conditioning too. Then I see these arrows that are incredibly judgmental. They say *degrees of difficulty*. Do you know how hard this is on me? I go for something around level zero, because that way you make more progress with less resistance. There's nothing worse than setting it on level eight and having this ninety-eight pound woman next to you going eight times faster than you. I'd rather go at a low degree of difficulty so it looks like I'm in really great shape.

Have you seen those programs designed to help work your cardiovascular system, and they are programmed to give you commands and be rude to you? The machine begins to mock you: "Go faster." I'm like, "You go faster!"

Then it says, "Reverse your direction and go backward." I'm going backward and losing all the momentum I've worked for.

Then it tries to test your intelligence—I mean, agility. "Pull with your arms; now push with your arms." What's the difference? I am pushing and pulling at the same time. And why doesn't it bother to remind me to breathe or compliment me on how hard I'm breathing? Yet somehow that machine knows things I don't know. It knows that when you pull with your arms you're using certain muscles, and when you push with your arms you're working different muscles.

Strangely enough, this is what a life of expectation is like. When you expect, it pulls you forward through inspiration and optimism and pushes you forward through confidence and courage. Expectation propels you forward—sometimes it pulls you and sometimes it pushes you. Faith pushes you to pursue a God-sized dream, and hope pulls and inspires you to never quit until it is a reality. When we live lives of expectation, we are guided by faith and driven by hope to do nothing less than create the future.

Now what you have to ask yourself is this: am I willing to move from what I have to what I could create? Am I willing to give up what I know for what I don't know? Do I keep shrinking back to the life I have because it's the default mode for existence? Am I willing to risk everything I have to create the life you could have? This is the same tough choice that those who came before us and were marked by faith had to make.

> By faith Abraham, when called to go to a place he would later receive as his inheritance, obeyed and went, even though he did not know where he was going. By faith he made his home in the Promised Land like a stranger in a foreign country; he lived in tents, as did Isaac and Jacob, who were heirs with him of the same promise. For he was looking forward to the city with foundations, whose architect and builder is God.

What was God asking Abraham to surrender? What kind of life was God calling him to relinquish? There is no evidence that Abraham was a bad guy—no story here of Abraham the mass murderer. Abraham wasn't a corrupt, greedy landowner who needed to get his life in order. All we are told is that Abraham lived in one place where he had security and certainty, and God said, "I want you to give up everything you have, everything you know, and relinquish your security and certainty. I want you to expect more. And I want you to go with me on a journey to a place you have no idea where it is, no idea what it's going to be like, and I want you to move from being a settler to becoming a stranger and a wanderer."

Creating the life of your dreams probably isn't about leaving a life of crime and reforming into an ideal citizen. Most of us haven't been that inventive in our sinfulness. It's really about leaving a life of security and certainty and expecting more from the life that God created you to live. I wonder if for many of us, the only thing stopping us from living the life God created us to live—the life of our dreams—is to let go of a life so good that it betrays the great. Are we willing to give up all the things we have right now to be able to obtain that which God longs for us tomorrow?

Abraham was simply asked to leave a good life so that he might receive God's best for him. It would not have been unreasonable for Abraham to say, "God, I'll worship you, but from here. I'll acknowledge you, but I'm not going to destabilize my family; I've worked too hard for all this; I'm not taking my faith on the road."

WORTH THE RISK

Are you settling for a life that puts you to sleep? Wouldn't it be better to dream with your eyes open? Is the only reason you keep your job because it's the one you've got? The only reason you have your career is because it made sense at the time? I think a lot of us are not on a path; we're in a rut. We have confused comfort with peace, belief with faith, safety with wisdom, wealth with blessing, and existence with life. And for many of us, our dreams will be buried under the epitaph, "I refused to let go of what I had."

To achieve great things, we must be willing to make great sacrifices. We see this played out clearly in the life of Moses.

By faith Moses, when he had grown up, refused to be known as the son of Pharaoh's daughter. He chose to be mistreated along with the people of God rather than to enjoy the fleeting pleasures of sin. He regarded disgrace for the sake of Christ as greater value than the treasures of Egypt, because he was looking ahead to his reward.

By faith he left Egypt, not fearing the king's anger; he persevered because he saw him who is invisible.

See the pattern? Abraham had a stable life, but God called him to walk away from it all and move into a new frontier. *Give up the present for the future; believe that tomorrow can be better than today. Trust me, the unknown is worth leaving all you know. Lean forward; do not shrink back. Expect more.*

Now with Moses, it wasn't security and stability he had to let go; it was wealth and power, which is about as unexpected as a plot twist could get. I mean, talk about crazy luck. Every other boy from Moses' generation was wiped out, but he survived. His mother put him in that little boat on the Nile, and he avoided the massacre of the Hebrew boys. Pharaoh's daughter found him and made him as her own child. Talk about being in the right place at the right time. Who would ever have guessed that would happen—the very people trying to kill you end up adopting you?

Moses grows up as the son of Pharaoh's daughter. He is positioned to become a leader of the very empire that massacred his own people, and now he has a choice to make. He has to renounce being the son of Pharaoh's daughter and give up all the wealth and treasures of being the prince of Egypt. And for what? To be identified with a people who were slaves. Oh, let's think . . . son of Pharaoh, or slave of Pharaoh? Hard call, isn't it? Yet the Bible says it was for him to choose.

The writer of Hebrews connects Moses' choice to the purpose of God in what Jesus came to do generations later. Long before Jesus ever walked this earth, we are told that Moses regarded disgrace for the sake of Christ as of greater value than the treasures of Egypt because he was looking ahead for his reward.

Moses was leaning forward toward the future rather than holding on to the past. For him the choice was a tough one. He had to give up more than most of us will ever have. He could have so easily reframed the story. "Well, God, it was you who saved my life. You are the one who put me in the hands of Pharaoh's daughter. You, God, raised me up as the son of Pharaoh. You have positioned me with great power and extraordinary wealth. Think of all the good I could do for your people from the inside. Lord, you should rethink this. You don't want to lose this opportunity. I can work my way up as an insider. Think of all the time invested to throw it all away now."

But God calls him out and says basically, "You are right, Moses; I did all that for you. I have provided all this for you. Now I am asking you to give it all up for me. You can settle for all you have, but you should expect more. Rather than the son of Pharaoh, I'm going to make you as a son of the living God. Rather than being a subordinate in a corrupt empire, I am going to make you the founder of a nation that will be identified with the Messiah, the Son of God. Your choice, Moses."

The great challenge for many of us is that there will be times in our lives when God will say, "I have done all of this for you. I have provided for you tremendously, but I want you now to give that up for the life you were created to live. There's more than this." It is very likely that the life God has given you as a gift today is the very thing he will ask of you as a *sacrifice* tomorrow.

That was the challenge for Kim and me when we were in Dallas. For the first ten years of our marriage, my average income was about eight thousand dollars per year. I was really raking it in, bringing in great income for our family. Together we probably made about twenty thousand dollars a year for a family income.

We were not simply working among the poor; we were poor. It never occurred to me we could have applied for welfare. We just served God, enjoyed life, and slept on the floor. And we had a great time. This was the life of our dreams. We were dreaming with our eyes wide open.

Then everything changed. One day I received a job offer that allowed me to keep doing what I had been doing for free and actually get paid. We had all of this income coming in, and God was blessing us in a new and unexpected way. It was amazing. We were more than happy poor, and now we could buy a house—not to mention a bed. We were genuinely thankful. This was like the stories in the Bible. We bought a new house; we bought a new car. Life was good. That lasted for less than three years. And then we sensed the Lord speaking to us. It was a new and exciting invitation: "Give it all up and move to L.A."

This begged the question, "What do you mean by it *all*?" It was a huge test of our faith, but our hearts were filled with expectation. We sold our house and moved into a little place in a highly volatile community. One day Kim watched someone steal from the store behind our house and use our backyard as the escape route. We had more roaches than we had loose change. And you had to wonder, is it supposed to be like this? In most of the stories you hear about heroic journeys of faith, people start at the bottom and finish at the top. You're not supposed to get on the top and then drop off a cliff on the other side.

Sometimes God does so much in our lives that when he wants to work in a new way we resist, ironically, because we have become so attached to all he has brought to us. What can happen is that the things God has blessed us with become an anchor that keeps us grounded ashore rather than launching us out into his dream for us. Kim and I would have never experienced all the wonderful things God had for us if we had held on to what we had simply because we couldn't see what was coming.

Moses couldn't see that he would be the leader of a nation. He could only see he would be giving up being the heir of an empire to become a voice for a people. But for Moses there wasn't a future in it. It wasn't what God had for him. He gave up a future he could see for a future that was unseen. The unknown with God is always better than the known without him. Moses would not shrink back because he expected more. Once God had spoken, all Moses could do was go forward.

For all of us who dream of a life bigger than ourselves, there is a tribe who has gone before us. There have been men and women who have both expected and lived lives that seemed too big for one person. Their lives inspire us all. From Mother Teresa, who became the mother of Calcutta's forgotten, to unnamed moms who sacrifice for others every day. From Rosa Parks, who refused to go to the back of the bus, to my friend Rosa, who raised two children in poverty with the added challenge of being a double amputee. From Martin Luther King Jr., who gave his life for a dream, to my team member Marcus Goodloe, who out of the poverty of south central Los Angeles, raised by a single mom, is not only living that dream but is making sure it happens for others.

It matters that they came before us, that we are the tribe that doesn't shrink back.

No Guarantees Needed

After pointing to the better-known heroes of faith, a momentum builds:

And what more shall I say? I do not have time to tell about Gideon, Barak, Samson and Jephthah, about David and Samuel and the prophets, who through faith conquered kingdoms, administered justice, and gained what was promised; who shut the mouths of lions, quenched the fury of the flames, and escaped the edge of the sword; whose weakness was turned to strength; and who became powerful in battle and routed foreign armies. Women received back their dead, raised to life again.

There are some of you who will be for the rest of us an extraordinary example of the power of God to prevail in any crisis. Your life will be unexplainable. You will conquer kingdoms and administer justice. You will live out promises from God that will give us all hope. You will shut the mouths of lions. You will survive moments where you should have been dead, but you're not. You'll quench the fury of the flames and escape the edge of the sword, and your story will be that God took your weakness and turned it into strength. You'll become powerful in battle and rout foreign armies and thwart death over and over again. There will be miracles that mark your life that others will find unbelievable, because you expected God to do great things.

Now here's the reality: not everyone gets that story. There is another side to faith, another story of those who live lives of expectation.

There were others who were tortured, refusing to be released—not that they couldn't get released, but they *refused*—so that they might gain an even better resurrection. Some faced jeers and flogging, and even chains and imprisonment. They were put to death by stoning, they were sawed in two; they were killed by the sword. They went about in sheepskins and goatskins, destitute, persecuted and mistreated—the world was not worthy of them. They wandered in deserts and mountains and in caves and holes in the ground.

These two scenarios are not a contradiction to God. He never intended all of our lives to be the same. God's promise is not that everything will go well for us but that our lives will be well lived.

These were all commended for their faith, yet none of them received what had been promised. God had planned something better for us so that only together with us would they be made perfect.

For some, shrinking back means settling for safety and security, or pursuing a measure of success only defined by others. What you have in this brief but vivid description are men and women who lived their unique lives and took the path God called them, and no one else, to live. A life of expectation sometimes brings great public success, but sometimes God glorifies himself and finds the greatest honor from our lives when we are willing to fail in the eyes of others simply by doing what is right even if it means losing our perceived value to the world. Faith is not measured by success but by faithfulness.

I picked up a book awhile ago because its title was so interesting: *It's Easier to Succeed Than to Fail*. That's a nice title about optimism and expectation. It's written by a really good man who loves God and has had tremendous success, but in the opening pages he makes the statement that God is glorified by your success and not your failure. I remember reading that and thinking,

I know he means well, but that just isn't right. God is not limited to your success and failure. God is glorified when you simply live your life for the right things, whether you succeed or fail.

There are some things that are more important in failure than they are in success. Some lives have greater impact in their failure than other lives with all the success they can muster. Are you settling for a life that essentially seeks the measure of everyone else's value of who you are? Are you a prisoner to the opinion of others, or are you willing to allow God to create the life of your dreams? Would you choose success in the eyes of others or failure that brings your life its greatest meaning? Sometimes we hesitate to choose the more difficult path even when we know it leads us to the life we were born to live.

All of those individuals mentioned in Hebrews were commended for their faith. All of them had the confidence of their hope. All of them had a learned optimism and lived a life of expectation.

I love what my daughter, Mariah, said one day when she came home from school. She said to Kim, "You know what my goal was today in school?"

Kim said, "What was that?"

"My goal was to be vibrant." She engaged her day fully alive, fully awake. She entered in with an expectation of greatness. When I was in school, my goal was just to make it through the day. It was a success just to stay awake.

A life of expectation isn't so much about what you expect out of life but what you put into it. The former is about feeling entitled; the latter about living fully engaged.

Some of us sleep through our lives rather than live out our dreams. A lot of us make our goal to exist rather than to expect.

If one thing is clear in this passage from Hebrews, it is that how long you live does not reflect how well you live. The

real question is,

were you alive when

you died?

Oh, by the way, you can be living your dream and crash into someone else's nightmare. We see this all the way back to Abel and Cain.

By faith Abel brought God a better offering than Cain did. By faith he was commended as righteous, when God spoke well of his offerings. And by faith Abel still speaks, even though he is dead.

Cain was the one who didn't have faith and he remained alive, and Abel was the one who did have faith and ended up dead. Doesn't this go against the whole idea of living a life of your dreams? This is one of those painful reality checks. The Scriptures are filled with passages where God promises us life if we will trust him with ours. Yet there are clearly moments where apparently the good guys die and the bad guys live to tell their story.

I don't know about you, but to me this is not only troubling but also irritating. The drunk driver who feels terrible but not so bad that he won't drive drunk again kills the eighteen-year-old honor student who has never had a drink. The doctor who serves the poor with her skills dies at a young age of cancer, while the doctor who uses his gift simply to accumulate wealth dies of old age without ever serving the greater good.

However we come to resolve this dilemma, we should be clear that God does allow Abel to die young and Cain to grow old. There are times the good do die young. Abel was murdered, but Cain could not kill his dreams. It was Cain who, though he remained alive, was trapped in a nightmare.

THE ETERNAL FLAME

To live wide awake is not about finding a way around the suffering or difficulties of life. It is stepping into the life God has for you. To live fully is not contingent on how long we live. Or even any of the measures we commonly use to measure success. Maybe there is something greater than happiness or prosperity, or wealth or prestige. Maybe there are dreams so powerful they are not worth living without. And there are dreams worth dying for. I wonder if eternity is best entered into from a dream. Is this why we fear death so much? We are afraid we will never wake up, that death is a sleep without dreams.

When we live wide awake, our last breath becomes the death of our dreams. It is only the birth of an even greater dream that will leave you breathless:

> By faith Enoch was taken from this life, so that he did not experience death. He could not be found, because God had taken him away. For before he was taken, he was commended as one who pleased God. And without faith it is impossible to please God, because anyone who comes to him must believe that he exists and that he rewards those who earnestly seek him.

For some of us, our challenge is going to be to move from a life that simply looks for security to a life that longs for significance. Some of us need to move past looking to God for only the forgiveness of our sins, and begin to live lives that pursue God and to live in his pleasure. Again, it's easy to settle for less and not expect more. It's easy to settle for wealth and status and say, "I have achieved it; I've arrived," and not aspire to live for more. It's easy to want safety or comfort and say, "Maybe there's more to life than this, but at least I've got this." It's easy to surrender not to evil but to average and to ordinary and to give up your dreams, not realizing that God is calling you to more. For most of us, the battle is no longer between good and evil, but between the common and the extraordinary—between settling for less and living for more. And when I say *more*, I don't mean more stuff but more significance.

I think at the core of our spiritual experience, our tendency is to go to God to be forgiven of our guilt and shame—to find some relief. Abel felt God's pleasure even though he was killed. He still speaks because he lived for what really mattered. It is easier to kill a person than it is to kill a dream, once it captures your soul.

Enoch walked with God, and then he was no more. God took him away. Be careful getting too close to God; you may not be here tomorrow. This world may just become too small for your dreams. Enoch gives us a window into what our lives are supposed to be about. What our experience with God could be like. We should expect more.

Your faith, your religion or spirituality, is not supposed to serve as a way to get God off your back. It's not supposed to be a way to leverage your bets so that maybe you can get to heaven when you die. It's not supposed to be just about some way to relieve your guilt and shame. Dreaming with your eyes open is about living life to the fullest and enjoying God and having him enjoy you. It's about getting God into your soul, your heart, and your head, and letting him show you the dreams and plans he has for your life. When an infinite God comes to dwell in a finite being, dangerously beautiful things begin to happen. It is here where you become indomitable. The fire within you becomes an eternal flame that cannot be put out.

COMPELLED BY BEAUTY

I was driving with Aaron, my son, and he put in a band named Copeland. I asked, "Is this Emo?" I'm trying to stay up on all the music.

He said, "Well, not really. It's just sort of Emo."

I was confused, so I pressed, "Well, why?"

He said, "Well, Emo is really more like a guitar and a voice. Besides, this guy is not too depressed because he's not saying, 'If you won't be my girlfriend, I'm going to commit suicide.'"

I said, "So Emo is kind of dark and depressing?"

"Well, yeah, I guess."

Okay, I get it. It's a musical version of the brooding artist. Ever noticed that if you're an artist, you're supposed to be dark, brooding, despairing, depressed, pessimistic, negative, and cynical? And then only after you're dead do people appreciate you and your art. It's not like I can't relate. For years I had more in common with van Gogh and couldn't in any way relate to the world of Rockwell or even Monet for that matter.

One of my dilemmas ten years ago, as Mosaic became more and more a place where artists were finding community, was feeling pressure to return to my former self—dark and brooding and despondent. I was trying to be careful not to smile too often, because people get nervous if you smile too much. You know, like you're doing something wrong or you're insincere. I felt all this pressure. I should have been seasoned in this because by the time I was twelve years old I was in a psychiatric chair. I was everything those artists required—brooding, angry, depressed, and if you asked the right questions, psychotic. I was Emo long before it was popular. I was way ahead of my time.

But I don't know how, when, or even fully what happened. I entered a relationship with Jesus Christ and started to have this Enoch-like experience: I was enjoying my life and enjoying God and expecting that every day would be rich with opportunity and every moment was exploding with adventure and wonder. And suddenly it was a beautiful life.

Mosaic used to have a newsletter. I would write a small article that no one would read. One time, I wrote a confession instead. I said, "I know this may cost me my job; you may never be able to respect me or trust me again; you may never again value my opinions or follow my leadership, but I have to tell you even at the risk of everything that . . . I'm happy. I can't help it. I don't know what's going on. I've tried not to be."

Oh, do I know how superficial that word is—*happiness*. But what can you do when your life is filled with expectation and you are delusional enough to believe that you have the power to change things? This country was founded on the ideas of life, liberty, and the pursuit of happiness. Just hours before writing that confession, I was standing mesmerized by the power of the Jefferson Memorial. Maybe that's just it; it's the pursuit that brings happiness. When you're pursuing, you're believing and expecting. It brings fulfillment even when the task remains unfulfilled. By the way, research reveals that the people most rooted or grounded in reality are those who could be considered depressed. Reality is really overrated; it makes you a pessimist. To be an optimist you must be a dreamer. You must awaken the hero within you that sees beyond the problem to the promise. I call this hero the Believer.

The ideal compels you to live as if it is already reality. It is in the most artistic of ways the pursuit of beauty. Faith is the determination to create with our lives what only our hearts can conceive. We pursue what we do not have as if we cannot live without it. I wonder if that's why dating is sometimes more exciting than marriage. Maybe our marriages would get better if we kept pursuing our spouses.

You should expect more. Jesus came so that you could squeeze out all the joy and beauty and value and importance of every breath and every moment you exist. And if you're going to create the life of your dreams, you have to learn how to expect, how to internalize optimism, how to begin to see things from God's perspective. Because when you first came to the light, you were not afraid of the darkness.

Little by little we begin to live in fear. We begin to be haunted by doubt. We begin to settle for less. We forget that we are not of that tribe. But in case you've forgotten, you are not of those who shrink back. You live your life leaning forward and moving forward. You live a life of expectation. Each day is filled with opportunity and rich with possibilities.

Others need to see to believe. You see because you believe. If only the rest of the world could see what you see—it would change everything. They would understand that you are not simply a hopeless romantic. While some dream to escape life; you dream to live. You see a life, a world, a future, so beautiful it takes your breath away. You must pursue this dream. It is what makes you feel alive. It must become reality. You're not closing your eyes to the real world; you're just dreaming with your eyes open. You dream and discover and adapt because you expect. There is a hero within you waiting to be awakened. You see the needs of others all around you. You feel the urgency within you. You are artist, explorer, and alchemist. You have all you need to fulfill God's purpose for your life. You know God is already at work. You are an eternal optimist. You are in the truest sense of the word a *believer*.

focus 5

THE SEER

As I HAVE BEEN WORKING ON THIS MANUSCRIPT, KIM and Mariah have been in Zambia working on several projects. Mariah called and sounded so excited and alive. She asked me if I knew about the rivers filled with crocodiles, and I said yes. Then she casually added, "I went tubing in those same waters." I expressed my distress, and she laughed and responded, "It's the barbarian way." (Referring to one of my earlier books actually dedicated to her.) I told her to choose the Barbie way, not the barbarian one. Before she got off the phone, she threw in, "I think I might move and live here."

Now with someone else I might hear this as a declaration of intent, but Mariah is different. She loves everywhere she goes and everyone she meets. When she travels, she doesn't just find meaning and enjoyment; she takes them with her. She loves virtually everything and shows interest in every vocation she has ever learned about. When she goes to the movies, she walks out with a new passion. She loves science and music. She loves journalism and jazz. She could live in London or Paris, Cape Town or Sydney—and now Zambia. She's not flighty; she's passionate. She is a kaleidoscope in a world of telescopes and microscopes.

Kaleidoscopes are beautiful, and they inspire us. Eventually, though, we need the telescope to see the long view of things and the microscope so we don't miss the critical details. Sooner or later, to create the life you desire you must begin to focus.

As you begin this process, you start at the dream. You begin to imagine—to dream and invite God to expand the boundaries of your imagination. You begin to see what God sees in you and the future he sees that you are yet unaware of. Every great journey begins with only potential and possibilities. What can happen as you begin to dream and imagine and to open up the full spectrum of all the possibilities of your future is that you end up just dreaming and never living. For some of us, the problem isn't that we don't have any dreams; it's that we have way too many dreams or that all we have are dreams. We just live in our dreams rather than actually live out our dreams.

About ten years ago, I took a trip overseas. It was a bit unfocused. We had seventeen days to get to about the same number of places. In those two and a half weeks, we went from Los Angeles to India, to Pakistan, to Cambodia to Japan to Hong Kong, to mainland China and then back home again. Not to mention all the different cities and villages and off-the-beaten-path locations we visited while we were in each country. *Compulsive* would have described our global trek, even if we didn't factor in the endless number of meetings we had to attend and conferences we had to lead, since the trip was work related. That about half the trip was spent in an airport or on a plane probably goes without saying. It was a case of frequent flier meets attention deficit disorder, or maybe the result of a sense of global responsibility colliding with obsessive-compulsive disorder.

Even the well intended can fall into the trap of too much "yes" and not enough "no." For too many, the opposite is probably the case. Your life is waiting for a passionate yes to anything. Sometimes we are lost in the overwhelming need. At other times, we simply find ourselves fickle in our passions, desires, and dreams. There's so much we want to do, so many possibilities, so many things that burn within us that we end up in danger of choosing a lesser life than the one God desires for us. We end up falling into the category of *dreamer*, which is often a polite way of saying "idealist who never actually does anything." You even diminish your impact and dilute your contribution because you care about everything. You allow your passions to dissolve and diffuse when what you need focus.

You essentially self-medicate with apathy to keep yourself under control. You took care of all those out-of-control, un-realistic dreams and passions, and now you're just like everyone else. Instead of harnessing your energy, you decided to conserve it. When a person's light shines too brightly, everyone else will complain about its intensity. You can choose to live with your light on pilot, or you can develop the power of a focused life.

Focus allows you to live a life of full intensity
with all your passion fueling your momentum
in a singular direction.
Focus isn't about less
but about more.
It is the ability to interconnect
all you are and all you do
around a central life theme.
It is the difference between being a diffused light
or a laser.

Diffused Light

Some people are naturally focused. For the rest of us, maintaining focus presents a real and ever-present challenge. This is how it is for me. I have to guide you from the dark side of this particular competency. But the consolation is that if I can grow in this area, there is hope for all of us.

One afternoon I was grabbing lunch with some friends of mine down in the OC (Orange County, for those who don't watch the new CW or former WB). We were at an event together and decided to enjoy a meal. One of those guys has become kind of well-known now. His name is Rick Warren.

While we were having lunch, Rick said, "Hey, Erwin, can I ask you a question?"

I said, "Sure." I thought, *Wow, he's looking for my insight. Rick Warren wants my advice. Why can't my wife be here? She listens to Rick. Maybe now she'll listen to me.* Anyway, back to the story. But instead of asking me for insight, Rick said, "Erwin, are you ADD?" I was a little hurt, a little wounded, a little naked and ashamed, without a fig leaf.

I said, "No!" Then I got that hot feeling of, *You're not supposed to lie; you're a Christian.* I remember looking at him and qualifying my answer: "I think most people spend far too much time focusing on the same thing."

Rick laughed, adding, "Oh, that's a different way of looking at it." Then he explained his question. "What I've discovered is that a lot of the pastors who are really effective tend to be ADD." I thought, *Okay, I'm good with that.*

Around the same time, an amazing businessman and the founder of the leadership network provided me a wonderful opportunity. They made it possible for me to invite ten people from around the country to spend two days together, just invested in one another's lives. I don't know if you have people who know you and invest in your life and journey, but a roomful of people like that brings a lot of insight and clarity into your life. The gift of this gathering was that people I respected would speak into my life. Of course, what you hope for is an overwhelming amount of positive feedback.

You are willing to suffer the awkward silence when they struggle to find any areas in your life that need improvement. But it never works out like that. That's not a dream; that's a fantasy. Usually, it's a journey from compliment to critique. Soon it becomes a pendulum between your strengths and your weaknesses. And, of course, you like the strengths part, but you're not that crazy about the weaknesses part. For me, it seemed like we went through the strengths part really fast, got to the weaknesses part at blinding speed, and spent a long time focused there.

Around the room, every single person gave the same input: "Erwin, your great challenge is focus, focus, focus." And I kept thinking, *What does that really mean?* Well, actually, my first thought was *I'm sorry what did you say? I drifted off for a minute.*

We don't live in a world inclined toward focus. Focus is almost countercultural. We aren't trained or prepared for it; contemporary culture barely facilitates paying attention much less helps us harness the power of focus. Not in this culture, not in the world that we work and play and live. We live in a world that tells us we should know something about everything. You should be a generalist, not a specialist. If you are from the Western world, you are a product of the Enlightenment and of the Renaissance. You're supposed to be a Renaissance man or a Renaissance woman. You are supposed to be educated in everything. You were raised to be a jack-of-all-trades. The Renaissance person knows about everything. The problem, of course, is you can't know everything, so you learn a little bit about a lot of things. You've been raised in an educational system that wants to make sure that you are well-rounded. So you took math, science, language, literature, and so on.

Of course we should all take math. Honestly though, some people are great at math, but the rest of us were there because teachers love to torment small human beings. How many of us really needed calculus? Is your job dependent on your knowledge of the Pythagorean theorem? Yes, it good to know where the Pacific Ocean is and that it is not on the coast of Boston. But few of us need an expertise in geography, or Western civilization, or chemistry, or many of the other subjects we give our childhood to and don't remember in adulthood. But you are the Renaissance man, the Renaissance woman, the jack-of-all-trades and the master of none. Even if you happen to find your passion at a young age, unless you have unusually perceptive parents, they will do everything possible not to let you limit your development by allowing you to be so narrow. You've been trained to believe that lack of focus is the key to success.

Then you go to college, and you have three, four different majors. You know what happens when you major in four, five, six different things in college? You get this newly formed degree called general studies. It means you were everywhere, all over the map, but you never stopped anywhere; you never landed.

Is it possible that you're still in that same regimen, that same training program where you lack the focus that drives you to the path God has created you uniquely to walk? If you're going to create the life of your dreams, if you're going to discover the life God created you to live, you have to learn how to say no to all the other options. And the tough choices aren't between good and evil, but between the all the equally good options out there that are simply not the right paths for you. You have to allow even beautiful dreams to die when they are not supposed to be yours. To make even one dream come to reality, many other dreams have to be sacrificed on the altar of your imagination. I love the insight that the word *decide* is Latin for "to cut." Every one of us is a surgeon. We live our lives cutting away every potential future we reject and giving life to the one we choose. Every choice requires us to sacrifice one or more possibilities for the life we have chosen.

EYE ON THE PRIZE

The word *focus* comes from a Latin word that means "hearth" or "fireplace", in other words, the burning center. The hotter your burning center, the more focused you will be in your life. The more you can lock in to who God has created you to be—your unique gifts, talents, passions, intelligence, all the stuff God has poured into you—the more you'll begin to understand your unique place in human history. A part of living at your highest level is developing the competency of focus—locking into your big yes, your mission for life. Focus gives you the capacity to say no to all the other great and wonderful opportunities that come and to say no to those devastating choices that will jeopardize your future.

I'm intrigued by every and any instrument that allows us to observe things. From a microscope to a telescope to a camera, with each of these it's essential that the lens be focused so we can clearly see where we are going. For us to get focused, we need to make adjustments. There are several experiences in the Scriptures from which we can glean a process for focusing our lives and locking in to the life God created us to live.

In Matthew 14, we are brought into one of the most dramatic moments of Jesus' time here on earth.

> Immediately after this, Jesus made his disciples get back into the boat and cross to the other side of the lake while he sent the people home. Afterward he went up into the hills by himself to

pray. Night fell while he was there alone. Meanwhile, the disciples were in trouble far away from land, for a strong wind had risen, and they were fighting heavy waves.

About three o'clock in the morning Jesus came to them, walking on the water. When the disciples saw him, they screamed in terror, thinking he was a ghost. But Jesus spoke to them at once. "It's all right," he said. "I am here! Don't be afraid."

Then Peter called to him, "Lord, if it's really you, tell me to come to you by walking on water. All right, come," Jesus said [which makes me wonder if we've limited our lives because we haven't asked Jesus for things that we didn't think were possible].

Peter jumped out of the boat and walked on the water toward Jesus. Now, Peter gets criticized all the time for being impetuous, and suddenly jumping out of the boat didn't look like such a great idea to him. When he looked around at the high waves, he was terrified and began to sink. "Save me, Lord!" he shouted.

So here it is again, Peter messing up. But before you judge him, let me ask you a question: have you ever walked on water? I didn't think so. My best understanding is that only two people have ever walked on water—one was Jesus, and one was Peter. So he's in a very elite group. He was walking on the water and, yeah, he had a technical difficulty. He was scared to death because he looked around and saw a raging sea and began to sink. "Save me, Lord!" was all he could get out. He begged Jesus to get him out of this mess—which is a smart thing to do, by the way. Instantly Jesus reached out his hand and grabbed him. "You don't have much faith," Jesus said.

Ah, learning moments. When you are about to drown in a storm, you're really open to God and to whatever he might want to say to you.

So Jesus asked Peter,

"Why did you doubt me?" And when they climbed back into the boat, the wind stopped [great timing].

Then the disciples worshiped him. "You really are the Son of God!" they exclaimed.

Peter's experience exposes the same dilemma that we experience and helps us understand why we lose our focus in life. We get distracted by our surroundings and circumstances and everything happening around us, and they pull our attention away from where we are supposed to be going. The nemesis of focus is distraction.

Peter saw Jesus walking toward them on the water, and of course he screamed like a little girl (my apologies to any little girls). Jesus said, "Don't be afraid." Peter raised the bar: "All right, Lord, if it's you, tell me to come." So he stepped out of the boat, and he walked on the water. Now I think that's very impressive. I don't know about you, but if I walked one step on the water, I would imagine that my faith would be greatly enhanced. How about you? If you walked two steps on the water, you might really believe in God then. Three steps, I bet you'd start dancing; you'd be dancing with the stars, or under them, or dancing with the One who created them. It's this amazing moment, but instead of having his faith increased, something happened, and Peter lost his way and began to drown. The stuff going on around him pulled his focus away from Jesus.

Now the translators, they're trying to help us. It says here that when Peter "looked around at the high waves, he was terrified and began to sink." Now I want to give the translators a break here, but truth be told, they didn't translate what's actually there. If you look at the original language, it actually doesn't say when Peter saw the high waves. You know what it says? It says when he saw the wind. But when the translators read the Greek, which says he saw the wind, I know what they were thinking: *That's not going to make sense to the reader, so let's translate this in a way that makes sense to everyone.* No one is going to believe that Peter saw the wind; what he saw was the high waves, the effects of the wind. So they are helping us, except for one thing—sometimes the part that's hard to believe is the part you need to believe.

What the original language actually says here is that Peter took his eyes off God because he "saw the wind," which I know even for the best of us suspends belief. Yet there is an important insight here for us. Have you ever felt that the problem in your faith is God isn't tangible enough? Maybe you've thought something like, *If I could see God, then I would never lose my faith in him. If I could hear God's voice, then I would never fall away.* Have you ever said, "God, I'm all yours; I'm sold-out; I'm fully committed," and then a few minutes later you are distracted? The reason is simple. That stuff is right in front of you. It's in your face—the job, the bills, the kids, the career, the game. If you could just see Jesus, you wouldn't get so easily distracted.

But Peter could see Jesus, and it didn't help. And to make it more laced with irony, what distracted him was that he saw something that was invisible—he saw the *wind*. Here we find the exact opposite situation. It still didn't matter. He still lost sight of where God was leading him and allowed his circumstance to pull him off course. When Peter took his eyes off Jesus, his life potential was diminished, and he began drowning in his inadequacy. As talented as you may be, you cannot walk the road God has prepared for you without him. To follow him is to live in his strength.

When Peter took his eyes off Jesus, he was overwhelmed not by the storm but by his fear. Peter went further than everyone else, but not as far as he could have gone. How far could you go if you stay focused? Where could you go if you did not allow yourself to be distracted from the path you are to walk?

When you lose you focus, you lose your way. Before you know it, you're drowning. You've chosen to exist rather than to pursue the dream you were created to live. Why? Ironically, because you need to see to believe. You're focused on the wrong thing. You need concrete evidence that this will work, that you will not fail. Faith, for you, is about facts. You fear failure and uncertainty and mystery. If you could just see God, you would follow him anywhere. But you can't see him, so you go nowhere. You live a life without risk. If you could just hear God, it would be different. There's no audible voice coming from the sky, but you can hear your boss saying, "Great job." You can hear the human resources department say, "You would have a great future here with us." If only we could hear God cheering us on, calling us out. You settle because it's impossible to walk on water, and you shouldn't be held to those standards. Not to mention the potential of drowning.

We justify our loss of focus with the excuse that God is invisible. You can't see or hear him; it's easier to trust in the world you can see and feel. But Peter had God visible, physical, tangible, right in front of him, and even that didn't make the difference.

Part of what costs us the life we are created to live is that we don't lock in. We lose focus because we become distracted by our circumstances. We get pulled out of the direction we're supposed to be walking because we start looking in the wrong direction.

WHERE ARE YOU GOING?

Do you remember when you learned how to ride a bike? Remember what it was like getting on that bike and feeling so unstable? You're holding on to those giant handles and it's hard to control. Why would they start you on such a huge contraption? You're moving side to side, swaying like a hula dancer at a pig roast. If you're like I was, all you're looking at are your handles and that big tire in front. You're looking down at the sidewalk; you're not looking up. You're just working that bike, trying to manage that situation. You can't figure out how everyone else makes staying balanced look so easy. You're just fighting to survive.

And then someone, your mentor, the person you trust, the person teaching you how to do this shouts something that changes everything. He does it out of concern, with the best intentions— he screams in a deafening tone, "Look out for the tree!"

You didn't even know there was a tree, because you're just looking down. As soon as you hear, "Look out for the tree," you look up. You look for the tree. You see it. And you know what happens? You lock in on the tree. You're doing nothing but looking out for the tree. You think back years later, and what goes crashing through your mind is, *How did I hit that tree?* I've heard that chickens are easy to hypnotize because their brains are so small they can only focus on one thing at a time. That tree, you were watching it the whole time. You don't realize that's exactly how you hit the tree. Because what you focus on is where you're going, which, by the way, is the first adjustment you have to make to get your life in focus.

You have to ask yourself, *Where am I going?* Are you going somewhere that would bring you the life of your dreams? Are you going where you were created and designed to go, or are you headed in a dangerous direction that will end up bringing you incredible pain and disappointment?

I've been preparing for a short film project called *From Such Great Heights*. The script requires my character to be thrown out of an eighty-story building. But due to budget and the difficulty of the scene, the filmmakers were going to focus on the beginning of the fall through a tempered glass window pane, and the landing impact, falling through the shot from above the camera and crashing onto a thin pad with debris. Our producer offered to drop a mannequin or have a professional stuntman do the stunts, but that seemed to miss the whole point. So on and off for the past few months, I've been training with a friend named Ian Eyre, who just finished working on *Indiana Jones and the Kingdom of the Crystal Skull* and before that *Disturbia*. We begin low and work our way higher each time. The higher I go, the smaller the mat appears to be.

On one of my jumps, I missed my mark badly enough for my leg to swing off the edge and smack the concrete. It was a very humbling moment, and the limp was a good reminder of the importance of focus. Now having my full attention and postured for a learning moment by the throbbing in my ankle, we reviewed all the important steps to successful falls and flips. Ian reminded me, "You always hit what you're looking at."

It's true in motocross; it's true in stunts; it's true in everything. When you start thinking about everything else you need to do, you forget to focus on the target.

It's so easy to get distracted by all the things going on around you. If you resolve to live the life of your dreams, if you refuse to settle for a life other than the one God created you to live, you're going to see the waves and the wind. And it's going to terrify you and you're going to begin to sink. You have to decide to focus and lock in on the direction God has called you to live your life.

This first step in getting focused could be described as concentration. Concentration is directing all of our energies and resources to a specific task, idea, and direction. So to focus, you have to make this adjustment—to concentrate all of your energy and resources on where you are going. Set your eyes on where God is calling you and don't look back (and certainly don't look around).

Your potential becomes talent only when it is harnessed and developed. Your talents become strengths when they are focused and directed. It is here where you begin to discover who you are and the potential God has placed within you.

Without a sense of destiny,
you will diffuse your energy.
When you are focused,
you are your most powerful.
A destiny is not something waiting for you
but something waiting
within you.

When Jesus calls us to come, he is calling us out into a future we cannot walk with-out him.

The power of focus brings not only the strength of concentration but also the power of convergence—it harnesses all your talent, gifting, skills, passions, intellect, experience, the whole of you and brings it all together to unleash your highest potential. Without focus, not only do obstacles overwhelm us, but we also become distracted and diffused by opportunities.

The Bible tells us about a man named Jairus, who was a leader of a local synagogue. He came to Jesus, fell at his feet, and begged

him to come home with him because his twelve-year-old daughter was dying.

As Jesus went with him, he was surrounded by the crowds. And
there was a woman in the crowd who had had a hemorrhage for
twelve years. She had spent everything she had on doctors and
still could find no cure. She came up behind Jesus and touched
the fringe of his robe. Immediately, the bleeding stopped.

"Who touched me?" Jesus asked.

Everyone denied it, and Peter said, "Master, this whole crowd
is pressing up against you."

Have you ever been in a crowded room? I have stood in the
lobby of Club Mayan in downtown LA, where we meet on Sunday
nights as Mosaic, right when the five o'clock crowd is leaving and
the seven o'clock crowd is coming—that's a dangerous moment.
I've been standing on the steps wondering, *Do I really want to dive
into that?* It's a whirlpool of humanity. I mean, it's just flesh against
flesh pressed into a human sardine can.

Jesus pressed through the crowd and asked, "Who touched me?"
You can imagine his disciples' reaction, "Who touched you, Lord?
Everybody touched you, Lord." This is a moment when they had
to be thinking, *Man, is he becoming high maintenance? I mean, who
touched you, Lord?*

The disciples politely point out, "Master, the whole crowd is
pressing against you." When pressed, everyone denied it. So they
had to interrogate the crowd: "Did you touch him?" "No, it wasn't
me. I was just passing by, man. It was incidental contact."

So everyone denied touching Jesus, and Peter in frustration

tried to point out the futility of Jesus' question. But Jesus insisted someone deliberately touched him. He felt power go out from him to someone else. When the woman realized Jesus knew, she began to tremble and fell on her knees before him. And the whole crowd heard her explain that she had touched him because of her ailment and had been immediately healed.

"'Daughter,' he said to her, 'your faith has made you well. Go in peace.'" Jesus wasn't upset because someone had taken power from him; he was moved that someone came to him for help and found healing. Then it happened. This moment of triumph was interrupted by tragedy. This woman's healing had interrupted Jesus on his way to help Jairus, and now Jairus's friends came to inform him, "Your little girl is dead. There's no use troubling the Teacher now."

Jairus was brokenhearted. Jesus got stuck in the crowd, paused to look for a woman who touched him, and lost critical time. Everyone would conclude that Jesus got there too late. Instead, Jesus reframed the situation—"She is only asleep"—and then he raised the little girl back to life. Somehow everything Jesus needed to do, he did.

What Should You Be Doing?

We find here a reminder of the tension we all face—so much to do and so little time to do it. It also gives us a more realistic picture of a life lived in the presence and power of God. It is important to note that Jesus was extraordinarily aware of every time power left him. He didn't just send out power like a divine generator. Wouldn't you think that the best thing to do if you were God walking among us would be to just send out a general power burst to everyone who needed help? There are way too many needs among far too many people.

Wouldn't it be easier to just in one single swoop go, "Bam!" (think Emeril, the world-class chef). Everyone would be healed. Wouldn't it be better if Jesus had performed mass healings? Everybody is better. Why feed the five thousand? Feed the *fifty* thousand. Make it impressive, feed all of Jerusalem. End world hunger.

We have to work through the fact that Jesus did not heal everyone. He didn't make every blind person see and every crippled person walk. He didn't feed everyone who was hungry. When this woman touched Jesus and was healed, he stopped because his power did not emanate from him to just anyone. There was not just contact but a connection. His power brought her healing through her faith.

Do you ever struggle with feeling overwhelmed by responsibilities and opportunities? This alone can cause you to lose your focus. It's easy to lose sight of where you're headed and why you're going there when there is so much need and opportunity. If you don't lock into the life God has called you to live, you will find yourself pulled and torn by everyone else's desire and expectation for your life.

What happens to many of us is that everyone else has a plan for our lives, and we end up losing our lives trying to live theirs. Everyone else has something you should be doing. Believe me, if you don't have a purpose for your life, there are plenty of people who will be happy to give you theirs. If you do not develop the ability to say no to many important things, you're going to lose the big yes of your life.

Even Jesus had limitations. This is pretty unusual, when you consider the fact that he was God. I don't know if you've noticed, but there were a lot of important things Jesus didn't get done while he walked among us. He didn't end wars. I wish he had, but he didn't. He didn't bring an end to violence. Would have been great, but it didn't happen. Jesus did not end the condition of human suffering. It would have been an important thing, a good thing, but he didn't do it. He didn't stop the rapid spread of devastating diseases. It would have been a good thing to do, but he didn't do that. Strangely enough, though healing was important, he didn't heal everyone, and though feeding people was important, he didn't feed everyone.

What sometimes is hard for us to accept is that Jesus Christ, when he came into the world, didn't come to do everything in that moment. He came to do the most important things. He came to do what no one else could do on our behalf. Jesus came into this world and offered his life as a sacrifice for us so that through his death on the cross, we enter into relationship with God himself. While there were many good things to do, from the mind of God, this was the most essential thing to do when he came into history. Why?

Well, to begin with, he's coming back to take care of all the other problems later. In the meantime, what God has done is put the welfare and future of humanity in our hands. This is what God did at the beginning, back in the garden of Eden. This time, though, he re-creates us so that our lives might be a gift to humanity. We are God's strategy for creating a better world. We all have a part to play. For some, that part is bigger than for others. Yet all of us are critical and essential.

By the way, if Jesus didn't do everything, guess what? Neither can you. He left things undone, and he is God. You and I are not God. And what may cause you to lose your focus is not your lack of concern or compassion, or even your weakness or shortcomings, but the deep concern and burden you have for others. Your upside might be your downfall. You may just care so much that you're pulled in every direction by every need in every situation, and you take on responsibility for the whole world.

You need to ask this simple question to get yourself properly adjusted and in focus: *What should I be doing?* Every one of us has a unique and important role in human history. All of us have been created by God to bring him honor through serving humanity and doing something that makes a difference in the world. There is a hero within you waiting to be awakened. Some are born to be the hero of a story of epic proportions, others perhaps the hero for one small child sponsored across an ocean. Both require a hero's soul and have a hero's call. While you can't do everything, you were created to do something of incredible importance. The tragedy is if you try to be everything and do everything, you may so diffuse your effect that you will not optimize who God made you to be and what he created you to accomplish. This is why you need convergence. You need to bring together all of your talents, gifts, passions, intellect, energy, time, and resources and harness them in such a way that you focus on the mission God has given you for your life.

WHO ARE YOU BECOMING?

For some of us, the challenge is not being distracted by our circumstances or overwhelmed by the opportunities. For some of us, the real challenge of focus is that we get lost in uncertainty. What we need to develop is not simply concentration or convergence, but clarity. In this case, the question isn't *what should I be doing?* but *who am I becoming?* Self-awareness is one of the most critical characteristics of personal effectiveness and productivity. Do you know who you are? You cannot focus if your lens isn't clear.

This is something we see in Jesus at an early age. Luke gives us a rare picture of Jesus in his youth.

> Every year Jesus' parents went to Jerusalem for the Passover festival. When Jesus was twelve years old, they attended the festival as usual. After the celebration was over, they started home to Nazareth, but Jesus stayed behind in Jerusalem. His parents didn't miss him at first, because they assumed he was with friends among the other travelers. But when he didn't show up that evening, they started to look for him among their relatives and friends. When they couldn't find him, they went back to Jerusalem to search for him there. Three days later they finally discovered him.

As a father, I love this story. It makes me feel like such a better parent. One night in Los Angeles during our Saturday night gathering, I went home and forgot something. I got a phone call. "Erwin, did you forget something?" I'm straining to think. Bible? Backpack? Wallet? And all of a sudden in the background I hear, "Daddy!" Then it hits me, "My daughter!" I felt so bad. One of our friends brought her home. But now I feel so much better, vindicated even. I was only missing Mariah for a few hours; Joseph and Mary lost Jesus for three days. They misplaced the Son of God.

> He was in the Temple, sitting among the religious teachers, discussing deep issues and profound questions with them. All who heard him were amazed at his understanding and his answers.
>
> His parents didn't know what to think. "Son!" his mother said to him. "Why have you done this to us? Your father and I have been frantic, searching for you everywhere."

"But why did you need to search?" he asked. "You should have known that I would be in my Father's house." [That would not have gone over well with my mom.] But they didn't understand what he meant.

Then he returned to Nazareth with them and was obedient to them; and his mother stored all these things in her heart. So Jesus grew both in height and in wisdom, and he was loved by God and by all who knew him.

At the age of twelve, Jesus was not doing what he was going to be doing at the age of thirty-two. If you were the Son of God, what would you be doing with all of that power at the age of twelve? Showing off? Not a particularly good athlete? No problem, hey, you're the Son of God. You can impress twelve-year-old girls, toss around the fifteen-year-old bullies. Just think of the possibilities of being Jesus at the brink of puberty. Yet there are no recorded miracles, and the silence around the early years of his life are deafening with normality.

What Jesus was doing at the age of twelve was becoming the person that could handle what he needed to do at the age of thirty-two—and especially at the age of thirty-three. What you hear him saying to his parents is, you can always know where I am if you know who I am and what I am about. "Why were you looking for me? Didn't you know that I needed to be in my Father's house?" What he was saying was, "You should know what my life is all about. If you don't know where I am, just answer the question, 'Why is he here?'"

Jesus knew who he was, and his focus shaped his life from his earliest age forward. He had clarity about who he was, what he was about, and who he was becoming.

SETTING YOUR SIGHTS

Have you ever noticed that your worst decisions are often when you had to make decisions quickly? Have you ever made a decision you've regretted? Maybe you made a decision and then thought, *I wish I hadn't done that. I had to decide so fast. I didn't have time to think it through.* Maybe you had a lot of pressure on you, other people saying, "You've got to decide now. This is a one-day offer only. You have to buy now, or it's gone tomorrow." You're torn and don't know what to do. So you make that decision. After learning the hard way, I keep reminding myself, if I have to make a decision before I'm ready, just say no. I've made my worst decisions when I was put on the spot. Ever been there? Have you ever thought, *If I just had a little more time to think about it, I would never have done that?* You reinforce the old adage "look before you leap," or at least "think before you act."

While having time to evaluate a decision is a good thing, it isn't a luxury we always get. Sometimes you are forced into action—ready or not. Do you know what's even more frustrating about this? Have you ever known people who make their best decisions in an instant? They make really great decisions in an instant, which makes you feel worse that you made your worst decisions at the same instant. You made the wrong choices and they made the right choices, and you're wondering, *How could they make a decision so good so fast?*

Are they just that much smarter than the rest of us? That of course is possible, but mostly I suspect it's because they had a head start. Life comes at you fast and hard, with multiple options and opportunities and with endless variety and variations. If you do not know who you are and who you are becoming, if you do not have your hot center fueled by your core values, you will over and over again make wrong choices. Life rarely sends you a warning shot. You don't usually get advance notice on the most critical decisions of your life. If you haven't defined who you are at the core, you will find yourself making choices that lead you down a path you would have never chosen if you could have thought more clearly.

Clarity comes from knowing who you are and what really matters to you. We lose our focus when we are lost in ambiguity. It feels like uncertainty, but it's not because the future is uncertain; it's because our lives are unfocused. Of course there is uncertainty in the future. Guess what? We're all uncertain about the future. That's not the uncertainty that paralyzes you. It's uncertainty about who you are that blurs you—uncertainty about why you are here or what really matters.

Life ends up being more like a juggling act, and you end up with more balls than you can manage. You try to watch what you can control and hold those tighter. And in the end, you end up losing everything that is important because you don't know where those balls are coming from. But as you build your core values, you begin to have clarity and do not get lost in uncertainty.

When we talk about the will of God, you know what most of us are expecting to find? We're looking for a yellow brick road or a clearly paved one-way street. We want a straight line from point A (where we are) to point B (where we are supposed to get). We often think of God's will more as a tightrope than a compass. We want one path, clearly lit and marked so we know exactly where to go. We don't think of ourselves like little mice smelling for the cheese while God shows us the way through the maze. We act as if the spiritual journey is like God leaving little breadcrumbs, and we are Hansel and Gretel. Through the woods we can find our way home. But somewhere along the way all the ravens ate the bread-crumbs and we're lost in the forest, asking "God, where do I go?" The dilemma is that God doesn't draw you a map, doesn't give you chalk lines, doesn't leave you bread crumbs. He builds your char-acter. As you develop your character, you have an internal compass that guides your way and begins to give you the clarity to see the life of your dreams. It is here that the hero within you is awakened, and you discover you are the seer. While others may be lost in the fog of ambiguity, you see your path clearly for you know exactly who you are and why you are on this journey. The future is not waiting for you, it is waiting within you.

In the book of Hebrews, we find the final but maybe the most criti-cal area where we need to adjust our lens in order to stay focused.

Therefore, since we are surrounded by such a huge crowd of wit-nesses to the life of faith, let us strip off every weight that slows us down, especially the sin that so easily hinders our progress. And let us run with endurance the race that God has set before us. We do this by keeping our eyes on Jesus, on whom our faith depends from start to finish. He was willing to die a shameful death on the cross because of the joy he knew would be his afterward. Now he is seated in the place of highest honor beside God's throne in heaven. Think about all he endured when sinful people did such terrible things to him, so that you don't become weary and give up.

The writer of Hebrews is giving us a warning. Just after listing several inspiring examples of individuals who were fully alive, he cautions us and gives us a process to avoid losing the life we were created to live. "Let us strip off every weight that slows us down, especially the sin that so easily hinders our progress. And let us run with endurance the race that God has set before us. We do this by keeping our eyes on Jesus, on whom our faith depends from start to finish" (vv. 1–2).

Sometimes we need to focus by concentrating on where God is calling us and not getting distracted by external pressures, circumstances, struggles, and problems. We need to focus all of who we are until we have the convergence of all our energies and refuse to be overwhelmed by all the options out there. We need to ask not only *where am I going?* and w*hat should I be doing?* but also *who am I becoming?*

It might be that the most critical thing we can do to develop focus is to have clarity about our identity by answering these questions: Who has God created me to be? What has God created me to do? Then we begin to build our cores so we can make good decisions in an instant.

It may be that you need to clean your lens, because every lens needs to be taken care of or the focus won't really matter. Whether it's a microscope, telescope, or camera, you have to keep that lens clean. In your spiritual journey, the lens is your soul. The only way you can begin to create the life of your dreams is to see clearly, and you can only see clearly when you allow God to cleanse you from the inside out. I have a special microfiber cleaning cloth that both cleans effectively and protects my lens from scratching. There's a beautiful parallel in regard to how God brings cleansing to our souls. He gets rid of everything that impedes our vision.

AN EYE FOR THE FUTURE

Also, make sure you get rid of the baggage that slows you down. There are some things that will bring you to a stop, or at least slow you down, drag you down, and keep you from living the life God created you to live. And it's not all the bad stuff. Sometimes you choose the average rather than the extraordinary. Sometimes we are dragged down because we choose a lesser dream that requires less courage, less risk, less sacrifice. So we abdicate the great dream God has for us.

At other times, it's not the good that's getting in our way. The writer of Hebrews warns us, "Be careful of the sin that entangles." There's something inside all of us that really needs to be changed. We need God to clean the soul's lens so we can be able to see his future clearly. It amazing how negative emotions and attitudes like bitterness, jealousy, hatred, unforgiveness, fear, or arrogance can skew your view of the world, blind you to the potential of your life, and turn your dreams into a nightmare.

The focus of your life isn't supposed to be your shortcomings, failures, sin, guilt, or shame. Remember, if you're looking at the tree, you're going to crash into it. I think religion has done enough damage by focusing way too much on sin and guilt and shame. Yes, you need to be aware of sin. You need to be honest about it. You need to come clean. Yes, sin can cost you your dreams. Because what you have at your core shapes everything about the life you will live. And sin and guilt and shame are not where God wants you to focus your life. He wants you to focus on the unique nature of your creation—that you're created in the image and likeness of God, that you have infinite value to God, and were designed by God to live a life beyond your wildest imagination. There is a connection between being a believer and a seer. When you expect your dreams to become your life you find the strength and resolve to focus. When you dream, and discover, and adapt, and expect, your potential erupts like a newly opened oil well. When you add focus you harness all that potential and become potent.

When you have focus, you also develop the uncanny ability to see what others are missing—what others are blind to. When everyone else sees the world falling apart you see how everything is coming together. You see all of us—all humanity, all history, all the universe—as interconnected. Everything that happens in life is connected and your ability to focus brings it together into one story. It is not incidental to you that the word universe means "one story." You see beyond the moment into the future. You see beauty when others only see tragedy. You see hope when others only see despair. You see possibilities when others only see problems. You see others when others only see themselves. You see eternity when others only see history. You see God in everything. You are a seer.

create **6**

THE ACTIVIST

IT WAS A SUNDAY AFTERNOON WHEN GRANT SOWTER, a friend from New Zealand, and I were desperately trying to work our way through—well, really around—an endless line of hopefuls waiting to gain access to an old warehouse in one of the less desirable parts of downtown LA. The line of humanity stretched for what seemed miles. It was a poor excuse for a studio, and you could hardly imagine a Picasso or van Gogh gracing such a place. But it was the modern graffiti artist Banksy, and there couldn't be a more appropriate place to display his work or reflect his spirit.

It was strange because until that week I had never heard of Banksy. Just days earlier, a friend of mine, Scott Reynolds, who writes for Showtime's *Dexter* (yes, I know) came up to me and told me I reminded him of Banksy. I was hoping it was a compliment. He explained that my approach to Mosaic was like Banksy's approach toward art. Then that very same week, the Sowters had a layover in LA from London, and Grant brought me a gift—an art book on the life and work of Banksy titled *Wall and Piece*. To make it the perfect trifecta, Scott called to let me know Banksy was unexpectedly in Los Angeles in the rave version of an art gallery. Banksy's work is raw, unconventional, and countercultural. If all I could get was a glimpse, it would be worth it.

I love the metaphor of a modern graffiti artist. Most of our art is left to the streets. We will never grace the walls of the Getty or the Louvre. Yet our lives are no less a work of art. It just may be more graffiti than impressionist. The canvas is nothing less than our lives. Yes, we are all artists. We are creating works that reflect the beauty and tragedy of the human soul.

For some of us, it is a daunting thing to consider that we are a part of the creative process. We would rather think only God paints or writes the symphony. After all, he is the master artist—the Creator of the universe. He's much better at this than the rest of us. I agree, but that's just not the way it works. The Creator, as the ultimate act of creativity, has created you to be creative. This is both your birthright and your destiny. To create is in your essence and is essential for living the life God created you to live.

ORIGINALS

When I was at the University of North Carolina–Chapel Hill, I took a course on music history. While I have forgotten most of what I learned, the class left an indelible mark on my life. Working my way through the Baroque period and the Gregorian chant and twelve-tonal music, not to mention the classics with the likes of Liszt, Mozart, and Beethoven, something began to haunt me. Have you ever listened to music and wondered if there is ever going to be a day when no new approach to music can be created? One day we will wake up and discover that every melody has been written, every lyric has been penned. Everything becomes retro, because every style and form of music has already been created. It would become, as Solomon said in the book of Ecclesiastes, "nothing new under the sun."

It's amazing there are so many sounds and songs and styles of music. Especially when you think about the inherent limitation—there are only twelve notes. Out of these same twelve notes, generation after generation, culture after culture, century after century, millennium after millennium, we're still coming up with new sounds, new configurations. Jazz, bluegrass, gospel, punk, country, Emo, alternative, grunge, pop, rock, classical, techno, rap, hip-hop, R&B, soul, reggae, Latin, blues, disco, electronic, djing, scratching, beat box, opera, and the list (or the beat) goes on and on. Wouldn't you think eventually we would exhaust those twelve notes? And yet when you step into India or Tibet or Pakistan or Peru or Brazil or Kenya or Seattle, those same twelve notes are expressed in completely different ways.

It's the same with art. Wouldn't you think eventually there would be no more original paintings, no more original ways to approach a canvas? No fresh applications of sculpture or design? I mean there are only three primary colors. What can you really do with three colors? We are so limited. You thought twelve notes were limiting. Three colors, talk about having our hands tied in the creative process! Not for the artist. For them the boundaries are the parameters, not the limitations.

In architecture, all you have are lines, circles, and angles. You don't have much to work with: just circles, triangles, and squares. That's it. You would think eventually some architect would be the last one to get an original design for a building, but they just keep popping up, one more, then another, then still another. It's all about how you organize those lines, curves, and angles.

Last time I checked, there are only nine digits. I don't think zero counts (although the discovery of zero changed everything). Nine numbers. But you have an infinite number of configurations and possibilities. There are some things that seem to limit us, but this particular field proves to us that there are infinite possibilities, even though there is a finite amount of material and parameters that at first appear exhaustible.

We know from the Scriptures that God is the only One who creates out of nothing. He created the universe when there was nothing. God spoke and everything came into being. This is God's unique creative arena, creating *ex nihilo*—out of nothing. He is the One who takes the zero and from it creates the infinite. And by the way, in case you've been wondering, you are incapable of this. That may be the primary source of frustration in your life. You're trying to create out of nothing. It would be like an architect trying to design without lines, curves, and angles, or an artist trying to paint without red, blue, and yellow, or a musician trying to play without an A or B-flat or C-sharp.

Those who are most creative understand the core material from which they have to work. They understand it to such a degree that they are able to go to places other people could never imagine possible. The great artists, architects, musicians, and mathematicians understand that though there is a finite number of material from which they begin, there is an infinite number of possibilities.

You would think by now all we would be left with is duplication and redundancy. Yet the creative process continues. Think about the uniqueness of people. There are approximately 6.7 billion people on the planet. After a while, you would think that humans would start becoming redundant. How many different lives can there be, right? Eventually you have to start running out of options.

In this book, we've been talking about imagining a unique life, about living an original life. We live as if the possibilities are limitless. Yet millions of people have existed before us. Certainly by now there are no new lives to be lived. All the great lives and stories surely have already been exhausted. All that's left is to imitate. You're left to become a carbon copy of a life already lived. Yet we somehow know our lives are to be more than cheap imitations of another's. That wouldn't be living; that wouldn't even be existing—that would be torment.

All of us long to find our own unique path. Even those who are deeply devoted to Jesus strive to imitate Christ without becoming an imitation. We know the difference between the authentic and the cosmetic. We are also called to conform to the character of Christ and not to conform to the pattern of this world (Rom. 12:2). Both change us at the core and shape who we become. But there is a difference between them—not only in their outcome but in their intent. The world, as Paul describes it, will rob from you your uniqueness. If you conform to it, you will lose your soul. You will lose yourself. To conform to Christ is to allow the One who created you to shape your character. It is here that God begins to reclaim, redirect, and unleash your creative potential. To conform to Christ is not to surrender your creative potential but to fully actualize it.

CREATIVE DIFFERENCES

Why is it that our faith, for some strange reason, often inhibits us from developing our creative potential? It seems almost sacrilegious to say that you are creative. Yet if we think this way, we have missed the point—if there is any creativity in us, it is because the creator God put it within us. We have been told that only God is creative, and all we are supposed to do is obey. No wonder people outside the faith see us as controlling and dogmatic. We have also bought into the lie that we are incapable of doing anything good, which is a terrible misunderstanding of the Scriptures.

How could your God-given gifts, when fueled by a heart for God and a love for people, somehow rob God of his glory? You at your best are not in competition with God but in concert with

God. Take the word *creative* and whittle it down to its core meaning, and what you're left with is "to create." This makes you a creator, which of course is where the rub comes. *I am not a creator,* we think. *Only God creates. He's the one who creates out of nothing.*

You know the age-old question, which came first: the chicken or the egg? Well, whichever one it was, God created it. You and I, we can't create either out of thin air. But boy, can we make a mean omelet. And that's just the start—over easy, scrambled, sunny-side up, Benedict, hard-boiled, poached, and the list is as long as our imaginations and, yes, our creativity. God created the chicken and the egg. But we created quiche. Thank God for the French.

Religion historically tends to create a sense of fatalism. In this perspective, world history is already designed and organized and ordered by a higher power, and we're just filling in the blanks. The future is already set, the present is already certain, and you can't change the past.

In fact, I was listening to a trailer today for the Star Wars movie *Revenge of the Sith* that said there is one thing you cannot avoid, and it is your destiny. That's the viewpoint of many people. If you were born to be Darth Maul, guess what? Tough luck. You are Darth Maul. If you were born to be Darth Vader, that's the way it goes. You can do what you want, you can fight it, but in the end you are going to be whatever you were destined to become.

As a follower of Jesus Christ, you need to be careful that you do not embrace these kinds of fatalistic views and actually call them Christian or biblical. I thought it was interesting in the film *Kingdom of Heaven*—which I actually enjoyed—that both Islam and Christianity saw God on their side. Both religions were certain that God would prevail. At the same time, their underlying shared view of the world was fatalistic. After all, if Allah wills it, then it will happen. Or if the Lord wills, it will happen. I find this to be one of the most limiting frameworks for many people who believe in Jesus—they believe when something bad happens to them, they couldn't avoid it because it was God's will. And when something good happens, they're not really responsible for it because that too was meant to happen—it was simply God's will.

I have enjoyed so many of the writings of Paulo Coelho. I remember years ago finding his *Warrior of the Light* browsing through a bookstore in Italy. In it he writes, "God never abandons his children, but his purposes are unfathomable, and he builds the road with our own steps." History doesn't happen to us it happens through us.

I want you to consider the possibility that God has designed a role for you in the creating of the future. It's somewhat ironic how we are far more comfortable changing history or even making history than we are with creating the future. Every day, whether you recognize it or not, you are affecting the future. Every choice you make has momentum long past the action. Good choices create a better world and a better future.

Destructive choices bring pain and tragedy. Either way, you are creating a future for yourself and the people affected by your life. You may rather ignore it, but you were created with creative capacity. Your life affects reality. Your life today changes the course and quality of life in the future. You are responsible for your actions and the consequences of your actions. To be entrusted with creative potential is to bear great responsibility.

I think our theological fears about humanity's role in the creative process are because we have seen people all too often use their creative potential for destructive purposes. Our default mode is to deny the role of humanity in the making and shaping of history and even more so the creation of the future. We may not like what we are creating, but we are creating nonetheless. It's not about whether we are artists on the canvas of life; it's all about creative differences.

WORKING WITH OILS

There are least three aspects in the creative process that God empowers us to fulfill, calls us to accomplish, and holds us accountable to carry to completion. Over and over again Jesus painted pictures of God's expectation on our lives, and the responsibility we have for what we do with all he has entrusted us with. Let's follow his narrative over three parables, each addressing our role in the creative process.

After telling one of his better-known parables, Jesus drives home God's expectation of us and the reward of optimizing our God-given potential. "Who is a faithful, sensible servant, to whom the master can give the responsibility of managing his household and feeding his family? If the master returns and finds that the servant has done a good job, there will be a reward. I assure you, the master will put that servant in charge of all he owns" (Matt. 24:45–47).

When Jesus gave us insight into the kingdom of God, he focused not so much on what God would do for us but instead on what he will expect from us. Jesus clearly expects us to be fully engaged in this life and the creation of the future. This parable emphasizes the importance of attributes like faithfulness, proactivity, and initiative. If you're going to create the life of your dreams, eventually you have to stop thinking about it, dreaming about it, imagining it, hoping, scheming, planning, or even praying, and you have to actually do something. You have to act. You have to execute. You have to step into the real world and bring the change that you can only see through the eyes of faith.

A God-inspired dream isn't just an opportunity; it is a calling. Your dreams are not simply a source of inspiration but the stewardship of your life. If you choose to dream with your eyes open, you will eventually have to start creating. Jesus warns us that we don't want to be found empty-handed. We all have something to bring to the table.

The Kingdom of Heaven can be illustrated by the story of ten bridesmaids who took their lamps and went to meet the bridegroom. Five of them were foolish, and five were wise. The five who were foolish took no oil for their lamps, but the other five were wise enough to take along extra oil. When the bridegroom was delayed, they all lay down and slept. At midnight they were roused by the shout, "Look, the bridegroom is coming! Come out and welcome him!"

All the bridesmaids got up and prepared their lamps. Then the five foolish ones asked the others, "Please give us some of your oil because our lamps are going out." But the others replied, "We don't have enough for all of us. Go to a shop and buy some for yourselves."

But while they were gone to buy oil, the bridegroom came, and those who were ready went in with him to the marriage feast, and the door was locked. Later, when the other five bridesmaids returned, they stood outside, calling, "Sir, open the door for us!" But he called back, "I don't know you!"

At first glance, this parable seems so unfair. Just because these bridesmaids forgot to get oil, they're cut out of the party? Seems pretty extreme, a rather intense punishment for five people who were nothing less than foolish or irresponsible. Yet if the work of art God intends for you to create requires you to work with oils, you better have them with you. Jesus is driving the point that there are things we must get done before he comes for which he will hold us accountable. We must not show up empty-handed.

Have you ever been in a hurry or wanted to get somewhere so badly that you forgot something you were supposed to bring with you? I can totally relate to the five foolish bridesmaids. (If it were up to me I'd give them a break, share my oil.) I remember driving out to a speaking engagement, and my car was indicating how many miles before I would run out of gas. It clearly said I had two miles. The event was about thirty miles away. I was in a hurry, and I was running late.

I came to an intersection where I had to make a critical choice. To the left there was a gas station about seven miles up. I might be able to make it, and it was in the direction of the event. Now I don't know why, but I convinced myself that my car was underestimating its potential or maybe exaggerating the crisis. There was another station much closer, but it was in the opposite direction. I figured, if I don't have to go in the opposite direction, I can save some time. I was already late, so it was all about the conservation of time.

So I understand these bridesmaids. They're probably thinking they have to get to the party. Who knows when the groom is going to show up?

So when I got to the light, everything inside me said, *Go to the left. Take the chance.* Right when I turned, the gas gauge went from two to zero. Actually, there is no zero—just a line. My car flatlined. Fortunately, I had turned to the right station in the wrong direction. It put me about ten minutes behind where I should have been, but if I had gone in the direction I wanted to go to save time, I would not have made it at all.

We often convince ourselves that the fastest way to get somewhere in life is the shortest distance between two places. There are times and circumstances where what you did on the way to the destination is all that matters. Those women missed the most important point: don't sit around and wait when you should be getting something done. Simply put, before you step out of this life into eternity, there are things you need to get done. Why do so many people who say they are waiting on God sit around and do nothing in the meantime? Jesus concludes, "So stay awake and be prepared because you do not know the day or hour of my return" (v. 13).

There are some things in life that are simply out of our control. There are also things that only God can do for us. There are things that happen in life that all you can do is pray and wait because they're out of your hands. I experienced this firsthand when our dear friend Chip was diagnosed with cancer, and despite everyone's great effort and desperate prayer, he was taken from us.

What Jesus is pressing us to acknowledge here is that some things *are* in our control. We are responsible to be prepared. We need to live our lives with the knowledge that one day Jesus will come back and evaluate our lives and take into measure the opportunities given to us. There are things that are not only in our control, but also for which we are responsible and will be held accountable.

The only difference between these bridesmaids is that some had oil for the moment when everything came to culmination, and the others did not. The ones who were wise prepared for the future, and the ones who were foolish did not prepare—they just weren't ready. The parable is first and foremost a reminder to be ready when Jesus comes and calls us to account for our lives.

Yet Jesus makes a powerful statement into the culture of those who will come to the party—be awake (which is where we began this journey), and be prepared. I love the motto of Caribou Coffee, which I found up in St. Paul, Minnesota: "Life is short. Stay awake for it."

There are things you have to do if you're going to live out your dreams. If it were easy, everyone would be living at his or her highest level. Greatness is not simply the result of genetics but of hard work. Often, the person who has the most luck is the person who won't quit. To live a life that takes your breath away, you have to be willing to get winded. While God created through a word, we create through work. God creates by simply speaking; we create by carefully listening. There is an inner voice that calls and compels us to create. When we know what to do, we must then act on that truth. Every great life begins at the same place—at the beginning.

Preparation is the beginning of the creative process.

Maybe you have great dreams but have not positioned yourself to live out those dreams. You've been waiting, hoping, even praying for good things to happen. Yet you have neglected a critical part of the process—preparation. Great art doesn't just happen. It is the result of tremendous talent, divine inspiration, and a lifetime of preparation.

CREATIVE DEMANDS

If you're tired of being a victim of circumstances and tired of feeling that your life is less then you were created to live, then you need to prepare for a different future. There are two aspects to preparation that are essential: foresight and discipline. If you lack foresight, you are not going to live the life God created you to live. You have to make choices today that prepare you to be rightly positioned tomorrow.

Have there been opportunities in your life that you wish you had prepared yourself for in the past? For me, one of these opportunities came when I started writing books. I couldn't type. When I started typing one word a minute, don't you think I wished I had actually paid attention in school or taken a typing class or anything that would have prepared me for this challenge? So as I was typing away, I would think back on all the times I cut corners, and now I was incapable of doing what I had an opportunity to do because I did not prepare myself. I didn't have the foresight to prepare effectively for the future God would call me into.

While some of us are headed in the wrong direction, others of us may be going in the right direction but we're not stopping and getting gas for the long haul. Are you living as if it's God's responsibility to make sure you have oil for your lamp? Maybe you're spiritualizing your lack of preparation: "If God wants it to happen, it will happen," or "I'm just waiting on God." When we fail, when we blow it, when we fall short because we were unprepared for an opportunity, we blow it off and say, "Well, that must have been the Lord's will." That's a Christianized way of blaming God for our own problems. There are some opportunities you were intended to have that you may not even see, much less seize, because you didn't prepare yourself for the future opportunity. Sometimes the reward is in the effort.

A young woman came to ask me advice about a choice she was about to make. She had been a NCAA athlete and had blown out a knee. The injury was before she had come to faith, and though she had struggled with bitterness against God, she found faith during this crisis. Her dilemma was so honest. She wanted to give basketball one last shot as a senior at USC but didn't know if her faith could take it if God allowed her knee to collapse again. "How can I do this without losing my faith and becoming bitter?" she asked. While her challenge was great and her fear real, my answer was simple: "It is all about the process. Make your faith journey about the hard work and the faith it takes just to try. Let your story be the journey, no matter how it turns out. You giving your best will honor God. Can you live with the outcome no matter what if you know you have done all you can? Can you find satisfaction in the power of this story whatever the final chapter is?" She smiled, and even before any words came from her lips I could see her excitement. "Yes!" she affirmed.

I don't know how her story will unfold, but I do know that when we prepare ourselves to attempt great things, learning is transferable. You have to look ahead and prepare to be able to jump in the game when God calls your number. Do now whatever you must to be prepared for the future you desire. This requires not only foresight but also discipline.

If you begin to capture a picture of the life you dream of but do not prepare for the challenges you will face to make them reality, you will not see it happen. Your future will haunt you like a restless ghost of the dreams whose death you caused through neglect. I see this all the time: people who have huge dreams but are unwilling to pay the price to see them through.

Let me just ask you, as you have been working through these chapters: are there some dreams that have been popping up in your mind, some dreams that have been exploding in your heart, some dream of your life that you sense, "God created me for this,

I know that I can do this," and yet you have not begun to make the life changes necessary to make it happen?

I overheard a conversation where one artist was talking about another who had earned a position in a certain artistic endeavor. The artist, who didn't even apply, grumbled, "He got picked, and I know I am more talented than him." Have you ever had that thought? That little devil voice in the back of your head that whispers, *I can't believe she got that job or that promotion, that opportunity, that role: I know I have more talent than she does.*

Eventually, we realize that success isn't gained by talent alone. Some people have less talent and are far more prepared; they have far more discipline and foresight. Some people do more with less talent than others do with immense amounts of talent.

If you want to know what your role in the creative process is, you have to ask yourself, "Am I prepared for the future I am to create? Am I living a life with foresight and discipline? Am I saying no to things that maybe give me temporary pleasure—not bad things, not destructive things, but just things that take me off the primary course in helping me become the person God desires me to become?"

I often hear about the dumbing down of America. We might assume that our cultural IQ is descending rapidly. Yet recently I read that in studies on IQ that the intelligence quotient of Americans today compared to previous years is actually going up. Why do we have the perception that it's going down? I'm convinced this is in part because we have so much opportunity and so little productivity that we conclude our capacity must be diminishing. We're faster, stronger, smarter, and have greater opportunities, but we lack the discipline to act on our potential.

The parable of the ten bridesmaids makes clear that God holds us accountable. He expects us to be awake and prepared. You can't be a light if you don't have any oil for your lamp. He holds us accountable to do what we are supposed to do. It takes discipline to become the people he created us to be. He doesn't just zap you; he doesn't sprinkle some kind of fairy dust on you or breathe on you and all of a sudden you succeed. Your effectiveness comes through the commitment and foresight to prepare.

Ask yourself, what does God expect of me? What is my oil? What must I bring for my lamp—my life—to burn brightly? What does my dream demand of me? And what choices do I have to make today to get there tomorrow? It may come as a surprise that a chapter on creativity is camping on the topics of responsibility and preparation, but if I am correct in saying you are a creative being, then the weight of responsibility on your life is immense.

BURIED TREASURE

Jesus then tells a second parable.

> Again, the Kingdom of Heaven can be illustrated by the story of a man going on a trip. He called together his servants and gave them money to invest for him while he was gone. He gave five bags of gold to one, two bags of gold to another, and one bag of gold to the last—dividing it in proportion to their abilities—and then left on his trip. The servant who received the five bags of gold began immediately to invest the money and soon doubled it. The servant with two bags of gold also went right to work and doubled the money. But the servant who received the one bag of gold dug a hole in the ground and hid the master's money for safekeeping.
>
> After a long time their master returned from his trip and

called them to give an account of how they had used his money. The servant to whom he had entrusted the five bags of gold said, "Sir, you gave me five bags of gold to invest, and I have doubled the amount." The master was full of praise. "Well done, my good and faithful servant. You have been faithful in handling this small amount, so now I will give you many more responsibilities. Let's celebrate together!"

Next came the servant who had received the two bags of gold, with the report, "Sir, you gave me two bags of gold to invest, and I have doubled the amount." The master said, "Well done, my good and faithful servant. You have been faithful in handling this small amount, so now I will give you many more responsibilities. Let's celebrate together!"

Then the servant with the one bag of gold came and said, "Sir, I know you are a hard man, harvesting crops you didn't plant and gathering crops you didn't cultivate. I was afraid I would lose your money, so I hid it in the earth and here it is."

But the master replied, "You wicked and lazy servant! You think I'm a hard man, do you, harvesting crops I didn't plant and gathering crops I didn't cultivate? Well, you should at least have put my money into the bank so I could have some interest. Take the money from this servant and give it to the one with the ten bags of gold. To those who use well what they are given, even more will be given, and they will have abundance. But from those who are unfaithful, even what little they have will be taken away. Now throw this useless servant into outer darkness, where there will be weeping and gnashing of teeth."

This parable keeps the intensity level up, doesn't it? If you're still uncertain whether you're supposed to be a part of the creative process, read this parable carefully. Not only are you supposed to initiate and create, but you will also be accountable for what you didn't do. All of these parables assume our capacity to be generative. They make clear that what God has entrusted to us, he holds us accountable for.

In these narratives, the consequences and benefits are extreme. In this parable, the master entrusts his three servants with three different amounts of gold—some Bible versions call them "talents." One servant receives five bags of gold; he invests it and doubles it. Another receives two bags of gold; he invests his gold and doubles it. Then a third servant is given one bag of gold; he takes it and does nothing with it.

Like the bridesmaids who missed their moment of opportunity, the third servant technically did nothing wrong. I'll never forget a line from Mel Gibson's character in *The Patriot* when he is being consoled that he had done nothing wrong in not defending the colonies against the British. His response was, "I have done nothing. And for that I am ashamed."

Here we find the second way we are responsible for our creative capacity. In the creative process, we are ultimately responsible for maximizing our potential. We are born with potential, but we're not supposed to die with it. Potential is not something you're supposed to hoard or conserve. The more you develop your potential, the more potential you seem to have. And time is of the essence. Urgency will spare you from desperation. You have no control over how you live, only how well you live. You alone are the steward of your life, and you must choose what you will do with the talent God has given you.

We have no control over how much talent or potential we were born with. A lot of what we take credit for is just a matter of genetics.

Just thank God for great genes and move on. For example, there are people out there who are far smarter than I am. It's frustrating, but that's just the way it is.

We may all be created equal, but we aren't created the same. There are people out there more talented than we are. And yes, it's irritating and at times discouraging. Yet someone less talented can accomplish more than a person with superior talent by working harder. On the other hand, a more talented person might give less effort and still succeed more than the rest of us. Life is anything but fair.

God may have made us equal, but he didn't make it even. There are some people who are smart *and* pretty, though we don't really want them to be both. Heaven help us if they're nice too. We don't want beautiful people to be brilliant; secretly, we hope they're really, really stupid.

The truth of the matter is that you have no control over the way God has designed and created you, what gifts and talents and capacities you were born with. A lot of that is in your DNA; you had nothing to do with it. You realize that, don't you? You have hair or don't have hair because of the genetics from your mother's side. So thank your mom. If you can eat whatever you want and not have weight problems, it's because you just have that genetic propensity. If you don't have that same advantage, it frustrates you because you wish you had a different biological composition.

There are some things you don't get to control. No one took a survey about my life. No one asked me, "Where do you want to be born?" and let me choose El Salvador. You didn't get to choose whether you were the ethnic minority or majority in this culture. There are many things you have no control over, whether they are advantages or disadvantages. What you do have responsibility for and accountability for is whether you maximize your God-given talent and potential. You have responsibility for your God-given capacity—that's the core of this parable of the three servants. Talent you don't use is talent you have abused. To waste what God has put in you is a dishonor to God and a disservice to humanity.

You have been entrusted with a great gift. Whether you realize it or not, your life is God's gift to you and to the world. Within you he has placed all you need to create the life that exists only in your dreams. Not to mention that he himself lives within you. This is at the core of your creative energy. God is the source of all creativity, of all beauty, of all that is good in the world. He places the potential for all that in you. Greatness doesn't happen in a vacuum, and neither does the future.

We have been taught that only God is involved in the creative process, but that simply isn't true. It's not true from a practical sense, and it's not true to the Scriptures. As I wrote years ago in *Chasing Daylight*, the choices you make today create the future you will live tomorrow. Your choices are not the only factor, but they are a critical part of how your future is formed. The Scriptures not only invite us into the creative process, but they command us to take responsibility for it.

CREATIVE FREEDOM

I have spent most of this chapter dealing with preparation and responsibility. In large part, it is because I am certain that for many of us the idea that we are to create is foreign and unnerving. Yet every day, a faithful mom or dad works hard in a kitchen preparing a meal for the family. It doesn't just happen. Some give it just enough attention to make the meal palatable and life sustaining.

Others see it as a work of art and make eating a life-changing, worship-evoking experience. Both are creating, but the latter are the creatives. You thank God for the meal. You know all the ingredients are here because God in his creativity placed them on this planet. You also know that the meal you created took skill and preparation and yes, even love. What others take for granted you understand to be a work of art.

If you still don't believe you're part of the creative process, then just sit at the table tonight and wait until God brings you dinner. Write me when you embrace the reality that you are created to be creative. Or right after you make yourself a sandwich.

You are a creative being. You are at your core a spiritual being, and your spirit is by nature creative. Creativity is the natural result of spirituality. This is why every human being has creative potential. Yet your potential will only be fully expressed in relationship to the creative God who made you creative.

We are creatures of creativity and invention and innovation. Just look at what we have invented: airplanes, bridges, computers, doughnuts, e-mail, fountains, gates, highways, Internet, jets, ketchup, limericks, music, NASA, oxygen masks, pencils, quilts, radar, spaceships, television, unicycles, violins, washing machines, X-ray machines, yoga, zero. Literally, from A to Z we can find creativity oozing from the pores of humanity. We just can't help it.

The question is not whether someone will lead the way in creating humanity's future. The question is, will you be among them? It would be tragic if only those with the worst of intentions believed they could affect the future of humanity. What would happen if those who believed in love, hope, peace, and the value of the human spirit also believed they could effect change in the world? We must embrace the creative process as our birthright.

In my Bible, I have underlined in each of these two parables one particular line. In the first one, it's "stay awake and be prepared." You need to stay awake and be prepared. You need to prepare for the future with discipline and foresight.

In the second parable, I have underlined the phrase "to those who use well what they are given, even more will be given, and they will have in abundance" (v. 29). You need to maximize your capacity, and that takes at least two things: responsibility and risk.

I love how the master celebrated both the individuals who invested what was given them and doubled it. I appreciate that he didn't say, "You didn't do as well as the other guy." You do not have control over how God created you, but you are responsible for what you do with it. What you do with your potential is your part of the creative process. I love that the master didn't tell them, "You invest in stock. You buy art. And you invest in oil." He just said, "I'm entrusting this to you; do something with it." The future was theirs to create. They were not expected to create something out of nothing, but they were given charge of making more out of what they had.

Some of you may not like this idea, because it gives you way too much control over your life, but you can actually do whatever you want with your life. You've been created by God to choose. I think a lot of us want to abdicate our life responsibility, even our free will. You get to decide what you do today and what you do tomorrow, but you will be accountable for your choices.

You may say, "I don't know what career God wants me to have." Do you know what a good starting point is? Quit blaming everything on God. Quit blaming your inability to make a decision. Quit blaming your indecisiveness on God. How about just owning up to the fact that you're afraid to make a choice.

It's significant that the master didn't tell the servants what to do when he instructed them to do something with what he gave them. When they multiplied it, he didn't quiz them on how they did it. He just said, "Well done, my good and faithful servant." If you are maximizing your capacity, you're on the way to living your life to the fullest. To do this, you must not only take responsibility but also risk. Why did the third servant bury his bag of gold? He was afraid of his master; he feared he would lose his gold and then be punished.

This is where many of us have been misled or at least have misunderstood. We're absolutely afraid of God. We think if we risk and then fail, then God is going to punish us. We are paralyzed by the fear of failure because we misunderstand the character of God. Life doesn't have a failsafe. Failure is real and can be very painful. God, though, isn't looking at failure but faithfulness. He's not waiting for you to fail so he can punish you or succeed so he can pillage you. He wants to celebrate your life.

What the unfaithful servant thought about his master was so far from what God is like. Even in the Old Testament, where you could agree we find a harsher version of God, we are told God finds no pleasure in the punishment of the wicked. He doesn't find any pleasure punishing the people many of us would love to punish. In the same way, he is not waiting for you to blow it so he can tell you how badly you have done.

If you're living in a way that honors God and taking great risks in pursuing great dreams, and you fail in the attempt, do you really think God is going to slap you around for that? Of course not. God is going to celebrate your effort. God does not measure success the way we do. We look at winning as the measure of success, while God looks at whether we lived. To those who are faithful to what they have been given, to those who use well what has been entrusted to them, even more will be given.

God gives you the resources and the freedom to venture out and do the most with your life. When our freedom has been taken from us, it is not God who has done this, but we have done it ourselves and to one another. While we may not be free in every way, we can be free in the most important of ways. Jesus re-creates us so we can re-create the world.

Every time you refuse to leave the world in the condition it is in, you are re-creating. Every time you extend yourself to make someone else's life better, you are a part of the creative process. You are adding beauty to the most important of all canvases. You are both artist and art form. You are a work of art and a maker of art. You are created to be creative.

Creativity isn't the luxury of artists; it is the calling of humanity. Because the world is in decay, you must create. The one who makes all things new calls you to do the same. Creativity is the natural result of spirituality. When you are alive, you will create—and it will be breathtaking and life giving. You are an instrument of the good and the beautiful and the true. You create not simply because you can but because you care. You are inspired by the prospect of a more beautiful world and are fueled by a passion that cannot be contained. You create because you must. You cannot sit back and simply watch life happen. The hero within you has been awakened and you are the activist. For your life is a creative act!

URGENT ACTIVISM

Jesus then tells a third parable.

> But when the Son of Man comes in his glory, and all the angels with him, then he will sit upon his glorious throne. All the

nations will be gathered in his presence, and he will separate them as a shepherd separates the sheep from the goats. He will place the sheep at his right hand and the goats at his left. Then the King will say to those on the right, "Come, you who are blessed by my Father, inherit the Kingdom prepared for you from the foundation of the world. For I was hungry, and you fed me. I was thirsty, and you gave me a drink. I was a stranger, and you invited me into your home. I was naked, and you gave me clothing. I was sick, and you cared for me. I was in prison, and you visited me."

Then these righteous ones will reply, "Lord, when did we ever see you hungry and feed you? Or thirsty and give you something to drink? Or a stranger and show you hospitality? Or naked and give you clothing? When did we ever see you sick or in prison, and visit you?" And the King will tell them, "I assure you, when you did it to one of the least of these my brothers and sisters, you were doing it to me!"

Then the King will turn to those on the left and say, "Away with you, you cursed ones, into the eternal fire prepared for the Devil and his demons! For I was hungry, and you didn't feed me. I was thirsty, and you didn't give me anything to drink. I was a stranger, and you didn't invite me into your home. I was naked, and you gave me no clothing. I was sick and in prison, and you didn't visit me."

Then they will reply, "Lord, when did we ever see you hungry or thirsty or a stranger or naked or sick or in prison, and not help you?" And he will answer, "I assure you, when you refused to help the least of these my brothers and sisters, you were refusing to help me." And they will go away into eternal punishment, but the righteous will go into eternal life.

This third parable is the most intense of three very disturbing narratives. Even if you don't know anything about the context, you could pick up pretty easily that you don't want to be a goat; you want to be a sheep. This parable gives us a very stark insight into what matters to God.

The opening chapter of Genesis gives us insight into this parable. It says, on day one, God created; then at the end of the day, he concluded it was good. On day two, God created; and at the close of the day, again he said it was good. Day three, God created, and then it was good; day four and God created, and it was good; day five, God created—also good, and then day six, God created and it was very, very good.

So here you have the rhythm of creation. Every time God created, it was good. The first five days were absolutely good—everything God created reflected his goodness. But day six was extraordinary—it was *very, very* good for one reason: he created humanity. The difference between the first five days and day six is that in all of the cosmos, in all of creation, everything God created could *reflect* his glory and goodness, but on day six God created a being that could *express* his goodness. There's a significant difference.

You want to know what your role is in the creative process? You are created by God to expand the good. Good is not a limited commodity, and God did not create you to simply siphon off his goodness. Most of us understand that were not created to be evil, but we act as if we were created to be neutral. Yes, God is the source of all that is good, but don't miss the point that he created you for good. God designed you to be an expression of his goodness. Every time you perform a loving act; every time you choose an act of mercy, kindness, and servanthood; every time you alleviate human suffering and bring hope and joy into a person's life, you've expanded the good and increased the honor God receives for creating you in his image. God loves when his children reflect his character.

I love this third parable because it tells me what matters to God. What matters to God is the good we do toward others on his behalf. Jesus paints an astonishing image: if you want to heal the wounds of God, you nurse the wounds of the world. This is how he divides it up. The goats are those who only cared about themselves, and the sheep are those whose lives are marked by compassion and action. However you describe it, they gave themselves to create a better world.

We might listen to this parable and think, *I have to feed the poor and clothe the naked, and all that other stuff, because any one of them could be Jesus. Then one day he's going to pop up and say it's me!* Jesus makes clear that the righteous people in his parable didn't help the poor to try to earn God's love or earn a place in God's kingdom. Their service to others was a genuine reflection of their hearts.

When you begin to create the life of your dreams—or maybe better stated, when you begin to live the life that God dreams for you—you take responsibility to prepare for the future. This is your life and no one else's—so own it. It's your responsibility to maximize your capacity, to take an inventory of who you are and to understand how God has designed you, to harness all the talent and skills God has placed in you, and to recognize that you will not be measured against anyone else's life but your own. Then you are ready to embrace your role in human history to create a better world.

There are enough people given to destructive and inhumane purposes and more than enough people simply content with living in neutral. But you want to live for more than yourself. You are a creator, and there is a future waiting on your action. You will need courage and compassion to live out this dream. You will only expand the good when your life is fueled by love and proved by action. It's not enough to feel empathy for others; you have to take some kind of action that reflects the heart of God as you serve the world.

When you look back on your life, how will the world be different because you were here? It may feel too big for you, too much for you to bear, too great a mantle, but you are a creator. Yes, there is only one Creator, but it's something to behold when a dreamer becomes a creator. If it helps you embrace your role in the creative process, see life as a symphony. While it is true you must work within the constraints given you—only so many notes and so many instruments—you have the privilege of taking on the work of an activist. You are commissioned to write a great symphony. It is the masterpiece of your life. You have been entrusted with this creative process. You are essential to this work of art—and the art requires that you act. You bring the notes that will be played. The symphony, though, is in great hands. The great Conductor will bring it all together, and the sound will be glorious. In the end, you are not only an artist; you are also an activist. When you choose to live wide awake you begin to create. And creating isn't an idea but an action.

When I think of activists, I think of people like Lisa Ma Perez, who demonstrates all three aspects of this practical kind of creativity. She's a medical doctor today because she paid a price when she was younger. She sacrificed many of the pleasures that the rest of us take for granted because she was preparing for her future. She's has maximized her capacity, taking all the skills and talents and intelligence that are inside of her and pushing them to the limit. At the same time, instead of choosing to use her skills and training to maximize her wealth—which others would consider absolutely acceptable—she chose to open up a health care clinic in one of the more impoverished areas in Los Angeles.

Lisa is a person who prepared for the future, maximized her capacity, and now continues to expand the good. She is creating a better world. She is living with her eyes wide open. It is no small serendipity that while on a humanitarian mission to Mexico, she met her future husband. Even while we are meeting the needs of others, God has a wonderful way of meeting our needs. When your dreams include the good of others, don't be surprised when God brings your dreams to pass. An example of young creatives is the story of two guys we have come to know as Steve and Steve. Steve is twenty-four (Opperman) and the other Steve is twenty-five (Dubbelclam). Both are Canadian born, and I met the first Steve when he was seventeen when I was up in Edmonton. They moved to Los Angeles a couple years ago with a dream of starting a line of blue jeans they had already branded as Iron Army. In their own words this is how it started:

> It all began about three years ago in Edmonton, Alberta, Canada, when Steve Opperman and I (Steve Dubbeldam) had just finished some overseas traveling. We never really set out to start "the next denim line" or anything like that. We really just started to get intrigued with the idea of blurring the line between fashion and art, creating wearable art. The name Iron Army was there from the beginning, inspired by a verse in the Bible, Proverbs 27:17 that says "as iron sharpens iron, so one man sharpens another.
>
> That quote is still found screened on the inside of our jeans. Now honestly, we were too cheap to spend money on designer clothes; we would head out to the local thrift stores and load up

on all kinds of horrible clothing. Then we'd take it back to our houses and start creating. We started patching, hemming, fixing, altering jeans on our Mom's sewing machines (which are battle scarred now). Not having a clue how to sew, we just mangled one machine after the other until some basic sewing tasks were learned. We also started to experiment with all kinds of crazy processing techniques from bleaching, sandblasting, dragging behind cars, grinding, painting, varnishing, sanding, and dying jeans using RIT ($1.89 at WalMart). Many of these ideas were horrible and ugly. But, a lot of the processes we were trying started to turn out amazing, and people got all excited. So then we began to alter our friends jeans for free—so we could practice on jeans that weren't ours.

All the sudden we were altering a lot of jeans and the gears started to turn in our minds that perhaps we should scale this whole production into a company of sorts. So we started to charge people $50 for breathing new life into their old jeans and also began the hunt for a manufacturer. After a lot of hard searching and dead ends, we eventually found a manufacturer in Montreal who was willing to produce small quantity production runs for us.

Our first biz move was to throw our launch party on Dec. 11, 2004 that we called the Pre-Release. It took about six months to plan because we made and did every thing on our own. Literally, we made coffee tables, change rooms, chandeliers, signs, seven short films, a stage, eleven projection screens, and more. It was a ridiculous amount of work. And on top of it we had to make two hundred pairs of jeans by hand! Let me explain: we got the manufacturer in Montreal to make three hundred pairs of blank women's jeans for us with only our back pocket stitching on it.

And then it was Steve and me to take those blank jeans and turn them into a premium denim product. So to make a long story short, we spent over $300 dollars at the coin laundry, bought our town out of bleach, ruined sewing machines, drank more energy drinks than is recommended and made two hundred pairs of jeans by hand in six days.

The Pre-Release was a huge success, we had bands playing, DJ's, artists, movies, everything. And from there it was time to hit the denim market. We registered for the POOL tradeshow in Las Vegas in February of 2005 and that was where we first showed our line. The response was good, we picked up some exciting accounts; but more importantly we met some key people in the denim industry in Los Angeles. After hearing enough people say "why on earth are you running a denim line in Canada?" we figured it was time to see what the Los Angeles scene was all about.

We packed up my car full of jeans and drove 2300 miles from Edmonton to Los Angeles. We stayed with old friends, made new ones, had all kinds of car troubles, slept in hammocks underneath semi-truck trailers, and eventually made it all the way to sunny California. The first day we got into Los Angeles the transmission on my car completely broke, just to add a little financial excitement to the trip. We slept on floors and were homeless for a good five weeks. During that time we were connecting and meeting with different people, buyers, and manufacturers. Then we made the big decision to move our production down to Los Angeles and start competing with the big players. We quickly began to gain some great buzz around our brand and picked up some key accounts like Ron Herman and The Blues Jean Bar. Iron Army was being sold in Barney's New York and internationally in Canada, Japan, Hong Kong, Australia, and Europe.

And if this is how the story ended, they would be a great story of the power of human creativity. But the story continues and not quite the way you might think. While Iron Army had great success in terms of two twenty-somethings with an amazing dream, it wasn't long before Iron Army no longer belonged to Steve and Steve. Like many start-ups, the creatives lost control to the investors. They lost their brand to the company that held the checkbook but their creativity was still theirs. So instead of giving up they did what had become natural for them—they got creative. They started a new line of clothes with an even cooler name. their new line is called [city of others].

For the past several years I have been wearing Iron Army. It looks like its nearly time for a wardrobe change. I love their new brand. It's all about the other. About bringing the outsider in, about caring for the forgotten. In fact, a portion of all their profits goes to serving the underserved around the world. In their own words, [city of others] is a company inspired to be what's next and will be known as industry leaders in marketing, communications, and in setting an example of compassion for people. What a perfect example of how all of us have the potential to be activists whose imaginations are fuel for change.

Maybe the missing component in our creative process is that we have not recognized that we were created by God to expand the good and that God will measure our lives by how much good we create with every breath we take and every ounce of energy we use.

God did not create you to be neutral; God did not create you to be a puppet; God did not create you to simply walk through life passively concluding, *Whatever God's going to do, God's going to do.* You can't create out of nothing, but don't underestimate the amazing potential that resides within you. The great danger for us is to leave all of the something we have been entrusted with and walk away with nothing.

To live wide awake is to take responsibility for who you are and all the talent and potential that resides within you. To live an awakened life you must have a sense of urgency fueled by passion and the courage to take initiative. When you become an activist you become proactive. To create you must act.

The Scriptures tell us that on the seventh day God rested from the work of creating. The first six days were a whirlwind of creativity. After, we are told God entrusted care and responsibility for this planet to humanity. It's our turn to get to work. It's our turn to get creative. It's time to move from hoping tomorrow will be better than today. It time to take your dreams and begin to create a future worth working toward. So how do you create? Where does the creative process begin? You may not realize it, but you've already begun. It starts when you dream. Then you must proactively choose to live where you not only dream continually but discover, adapt, expect, and focus. this is the beginning of the creative process. So go and be creative.

enjoy  **7**

THE HEDONIST

I JUST DISCOVERED PINKBERRY. I'M STILL NOT SURE exactly what it is—somewhere between frozen yogurt and heaven, I think. I know it's shallow, but it made me happy. I enjoyed every spoonful. Fresh raspberries, strawberries, and blackberries surrounding a mound of ice cream–like substance that is actually healthy. It's one of the ways I stay hopeful about the world. How can you not believe in God or in humanity's potential for good when something can taste this amazing? I know, I know, I'm making way too much out of an insignificant pleasure. It's much worse than you think. I am like this all the time. I enjoy life. It's a habit. I've tried to make it a family value.

When we were in Italy, our family saw—no that's inadequate to describe it, we experienced—the Colosseum, the Pantheon, Michelangelo's *David*, the works of Leonardo da Vinci, the Vatican, the Sistine Chapel, Venice. We went all over northern Italy and it was breathtaking, but my highlight experience was the gelato. At first, we couldn't figure out whether it was called *gelato* or *gelati*. I finally found out it's *gelati* if it's plural and *gelato* if it's singular. So for me, it's always *gelati*. We had one unifying experience everywhere we went throughout Italy—when we found a gelati shop, we would stop and enjoy. The goal was not so much our destination but the journey. And every time I eat gelati, I am reminded there is a God and he is good, and he has some amazing ideas that he infuses into the human imagination.

So many things bring me pleasure. Life for me is an endless

exploration of beauty and mystery. It's not that I don't have bad days; I do. We all do. But learning how to enjoy life when those tough days come at you is an art form. While life is filled with pain and sorrow along with celebration and laughter, the scriptures challenge us to find joy in every circumstance we face. Sometimes life brings an immeasurable amount of joy; sometimes it brings the height of frustration. At times joy comes as a surprise in the midst of painful moments. When you dream with your eyes open, you take time to enjoy.

I don't usually make it a practice to tell people what to do. I try to show them what their options are and where those options will take them. But in this chapter, I'm going to change my policy; I'm going to tell you to do something as if your life depends on it. I'm even putting it in print: I want you to go and enjoy yourself. Do whatever you have to do, but find time to laugh and appreciate your life. This isn't supplemental to living an awakened life—it's lifeblood. You can only give to others what you have. You have to be alive to resuscitate the unconscious, much less raise the dead.

There may be nothing more compelling or contagious than a person who is enjoying his life. If you know someone like this, you may wonder what he knows that you don't know. Perhaps it's as simple as this: that person has learned that life doesn't bring you joy; you bring joy to life. So the depressed pessimist who says there is nothing in life that can make him happy is right—which, of course, is pretty depressing. No one and nothing can force you to enjoy your life.

Others feel guilty when they're having a great time, especially if they consider themselves to be spiritual. Buddhism has become a huge part of Los Angeles life, and when you blend it with fundamentalist Christianity, you have a dangerous combination. From the Far East you are told true spirituality is getting rid of everything you enjoy, and from the Deep South you are told if something is fun, it will send you to hell. This could be the very reason hell looks so attractive when compared to religion.

When you think of the word *enjoy*, what comes to mind? Think of the most enjoyable experience you have ever had that didn't leave you with a negative aftertaste. What would it be? Let's focus on this a bit more. What moment in your life has brought you the greatest sense of satisfaction? Identify that moment when you felt most alive. Maybe you even thought, *I could do this for the rest of my life.*

There are so many things in life to enjoy—rain, sunshine, quiet, laughter, music, movies, travel, home, food, drink, exercise, rest, family, friends, work, play. If you are going to create the life of your dreams, you have to learn how to enjoy. One of the evidences that you're living the life God designed you to live is you begin to enjoy your life even when your environment doesn't seem to dictate that. Your enjoyment of life is no longer dependent on your circumstances. It is a part of your core, a reflection of who you are and how you engage the world.

Pleasure Seekers

It may seem strange to focus on pleasure for an entire chapter, yet I'm convinced that one of the primary obstacles we face in living wide awake is we are not enjoying our lives. We think that God and fun are mutually exclusive, that if you are deeply spiritual, you'll enjoy things less. The more you grow in your faith, the less you enjoy the things of the world. If you're at a Dalai Lama level of spirituality or have achieved a higher consciousness, or even if you're striving to be like Jesus, you laugh less, you smile less, you enjoy less. Being godly is apparently serious business.

In contrast to this perspective, what you find in the Scriptures is that God designed us to enjoy life; he created us for pleasure. God created us so he could enjoy us and we could enjoy him and we could enjoy life. God created us in the perfect environment for pleasure, enjoyment, and desire. This is the story of creation. This is our beginning. God created the world for our enjoyment. We took the fun out of it.

> Then the LORD God planted a garden in Eden, in the east, and there he placed the man he had created. And the LORD God planted all sorts of trees in the garden—beautiful trees that produced delicious fruit. At the center of the garden he placed the tree of life and the tree of the knowledge of good and evil.

In the beginning, God's idea was to put us in a beautiful place filled with delicious fruit and gorgeous surroundings—not to mention that Adam and Eve were naked. For most of us this is a terrifying thought, but factor in it was before cellulite went out of control. When we begin to enjoy life, we actually return to God's original intent. God never intended for us to live a life defined by pain, sorrow, loneliness, and disappointment. God created a very different world from the one we're running now. The garden of Eden was beautiful. You could see the sunset, and you couldn't see the atmosphere. There were no zone diets and no holes in the ozone. The world was designed to inspire the human spirit. We would wake up and want to shout at the top of our lungs how good life is. It really was a pleasure to be here.

Imagine waking up to a world like this. While that paradise is gone, we can still wake up to a world we enjoy. We were created to take care of the world, but we have not done a great job. Now we're called to face those problems and see them as challenges and opportunities. We don't live in paradise anymore. Now we have to bring paradise to where we live.

You are physiologically and psychologically designed to enjoy life. God designed you to experience pleasure. There are some things we are incapable of experiencing. There are sounds human beings cannot hear, but animals can hear those sounds. There are microscopic worlds the human eye cannot see, things that are so small that we are unaware of their existence. There are things in the cosmos that are so far away our field of vision cannot pick them up, but they are there. You should never assume that you can actually experience or observe everything that exists. There are all kinds of things you are absolutely unaware of that are absolutely real.

There are some things God created and designed you to know. You can see colors. God could have designed you without the capacity to see colors, and some of you are literally color-blind. That's not the way it's supposed to be—color-blindness is a variation of the original design. You're supposed to be able to taste all kinds of flavors, but some of you do not have any sense of taste. You cannot enjoy a good, rich latte the way it is supposed to be enjoyed. Chocolate means nothing to you, which is hard to imagine. If you can see colors, taste flavors, and smell aromas, you have the capacity by God's design to actually enjoy those pleasures. God designed you to enjoy; he created you for pleasure.

Have you forgotten that it was God who created you with desires, passions, and cravings? Religion focuses on the suppression of desires, the elimination of desires, the denial of desires.

But God redirects our desires from destructive outlets to creative ones. Religion is an attempt to control people by controlling their desires and passions rather than awakening and unleashing them. Consider the way we reinvent Buddhism, where everybody looks forward to being reincarnated. You get to come back in another life, and maybe next time you will come back as the next Tom Cruise or Julia Roberts. It's always an upgrade. No one comes back as a roach.

But Buddhism and Hinduism have never understood reincarnation as a gift; it is essentially a curse. You're in an endless cycle trying to get free from all of your desires, and the only way you'll ever end the trap of reincarnation is by eliminating all of your desires, which is the ultimate end of spirituality.

That is not what Jesus taught; this is not what the Scriptures teach. In fact, the Scriptures teach the exact opposite. While Buddhism says the ultimate act of spirituality is eliminating all your desires, the Scriptures teach that knowing and loving God awakens all your God-given desires and passions. The psalmist wrote, "Delight yourself in the LORD and he will give you the desires of your heart" (Ps. 37:4 NIV). You were designed to desire and to enjoy, and you will spend your whole life trying to find the ultimate fulfillment of your dreams.

Sometimes, in trying to satisfy our desires and passions, we go to a destructive place. We choose the wrong places to try to fulfill our desires. Have you ever wanted something so badly, and you finally got it—and then it owns you? The object of your desire became the beginning of your demise. You can become self-destructive in the pursuit of pleasure. This is how addictions become life-dominating patterns. Up front, most of the things that destroy us are extremely enjoyable.

This is one of the places parenting becomes very nuanced. You warn your daughter not to drink because it's really bad for her. Or you tell your son not to be sexually active because it's going to destroy his life. But let's be honest: all the bad stuff, the first time out, feels pretty good. It's enjoyable; it brings pleasure. And a lot of kids think, *Man, my parents said this is really bad, but it feels really good. They should get around a little more.* They are confused because they experience something exhilarating. What you meant was that if you do this in a way that demeans who you are and damages your soul, it will destroy you in the long haul—even though it's so attractive and appetizing and pleasurable up front. You were created to enjoy, but make sure you enjoy what you were created for. Your desires can lead you astray; "because it feels good" is not a good compass for life. We should make decisions that enhance our joy for a lifetime rather than sacrificing joy for momentary pleasure.

So what do we do? We create religions to try to stop ourselves from allowing our desires, passions, and longings to lead us on destructive paths. We create laws and rules and rituals and guidelines—not to mention throwing in all the guilt and fear we can muster. We try to control people with religion. But it doesn't work that well. And there's a reason we go back to where we were before. There's a reason we go back to destructive pleasures. There's a reason we go back to desires and longings that hold us captive. It's because those things seem to make life a lot more enjoyable than the life we have without them.

Rules or passions—which option is more attractive to you? Desires or demands? Freedom or legalism? Enjoy or obey? This last one is really important. Do you believe obedience to God is in conflict with the enjoyment of life? You'll never live the life of your dreams until you believe that God is the source of all that is good. God made you to enjoy life. He's not trying to stop you from enjoying life; he's trying to help you find the joy for which you were created. Your longing to enjoy life will never go away, because God designed you that way. But we are too often shortsighted and settle for filler rather than wait for fulfillment.

When there's a raging wildfire that cannot be stopped even when the helicopters drop tons of water, they send in specialized firefighters called hot shots. The hot shots go down and actually start fires, which seems counterproductive, doesn't it? The guy who starts fires without permission is called an arsonist; the guy who starts them with permission is called a firefighter. It's a little strange.

When there's an out-of-control fire, these hot shots start strategically positioned fires because they understand the only way to stop a devastating fire is to consume it with a new fire. That's exactly what the Scriptures say. The only way you are going to stop being pulled around by destructive desires and passions is to allow God to awaken those passions and desires that will bring your life to wholeness and health and make you fully alive. You need to enjoy your life because it restores original intent. It takes you back to the way God created you. You're supposed to enjoy your life. It's a command.

Pleasure Meeting You

But if we go a little further into this narrative, we find the second dynamic element of enjoyment. Again, what happens if you don't know the story, is that God creates man and woman, Adam and Eve, and places them in a garden. And by the way, the word *Eden* means pleasure. God puts them in the garden of pleasure. Think about this: Eden is an extraordinary place of incredible beauty and in it there is perfect harmony between humanity and all of creation. Every thing designed for humanity's pleasure. They were naked and unashamed. Imagine a world with no violence, no sorrow, no fear, no falsehood, not to mention no wrinkles and no body fat! God made everything beautifully and elegantly for humanity's enjoyment.

But then there is a break in our relationship with God. God then tells the woman and the man the consequences of their choosing to live a life apart from the one who is the source of life, love, and ultimate joy. "He said to the woman, 'You will bear children with intense pain and suffering.'" The pain of childbirth becomes a not-so-subtle reminder that we now are born into the world with a relational crisis on our hands. It now becomes painful to create life. "And though your desire will be for your husband, he will be your master."

And to Adam, God said:

> Because you listened to your wife [now, that's not a life principle; don't say, "See, the Bible says don't listen to my wife!"] and ate the fruit I told you not to eat, I have placed a curse on the ground. All your life you will struggle to scratch a living from it. It will grow thorns and thistles for you, though you will eat of its grains. All your life you will sweat to produce food, until your dying day. Then you will return to the ground from which you came. For you were made from dust, and to the dust you will return."

God is telling Adam and Eve that they have turned their complementary relationship into a destructive partnership. They will no longer enjoy life at the optimal level for which they were created to enjoy it. This is God's way of saying, "You've made a mess of life, and it's going to bring devastation in two arenas: in your relationships and your identity. You will spend your life trying to find love and trying to find purpose and meaning." But, like Adam and Eve, we choose lust instead of love, security instead of significance, and existence instead of life.

To the woman he says, "You're going to have pain in childbirth." And this is the cosmic metaphor, that while human relationships are supposed to bring you joy, now they're going to bring you pain. Anyone who would be honest will concede that the people you love the most are the ones capable of hurting you most deeply. A person you don't care about cannot hurt you in a profound way. It's the person you bring close, the person you invite to the deepest part of your soul, who can wound you most deeply. So in the most intimate moment—when your flesh and blood come out of your body—God says there's going to be pain, and this will serve as a reminder to you that there is a broken relationship between humanity and God, and it affects the relationship between all of us.

Then the next part of verse 16 is often used to justify male oppression in the home. God says to Eve, "Though your desire will be for your husband, he will be your master." And so many times we've told women, "See, your husband is supposed to be the master over your life."

God is describing this as the result of the world gone wrong. This is not the way it's supposed to be, but the way it is because of the brokenness of the human spirit. The Scripture is saying to women, you're going to fight for power. You're going to desire your husband's power, and he's going to want power over you, and the two of you are going to fight all your lives until death do you part. This is the War of the Roses. Time has only proven God right.

This is a description of the level of devastation of our spiritual brokenness. We have created a world where we end up wounding the person we say we love the most in the world. Even the person we trust the most will let us down. Marriage wouldn't be such a challenge if this were not true.

I know why many people are afraid to get married. It's because they don't believe someone can love them all of their lives, and they don't believe they can love someone for all of their lives. You're not sure if love works. We know this because we know ourselves; we know the hurt you are capable of giving as well as receiving. Yet as we create the life God designed us to live, we restore the pleasure of human intimacy and relationships. Part of living the life God created you to live is reversing the curse by enjoying marriage, enjoying intimacy, enjoying community, enjoying friendship, and enjoying each other.

Where are you in this? You can be married and very much alone in the world. Do you have at least one meaningful friendship in your life? Years ago, a survey revealed that men had only one friendship in their lives, and women would describe that friendship as an acquaintance.

You were not created to live your life in isolation, to think of people as disposable. Do you have any friendships that have lasted years, that have gone through turmoil, that have made it through crisis and disappointment? You will not enjoy life at its richest level until you learn how to have deep, meaningful relationships, because life is enjoyed best with people. When you look back on your life, the dark moments will not be about an economic crisis, the loss of a job, or even the loss of a dream; the darkest moments in your life will be when your relationships are a mess. And the moments you'll remember with the greatest fondness are those when your relationships were healthy.

Then God tells the man, "This is what's going to happen. You're going to work and work and work. You're going to toil and sweat, but the ground will be like a curse to you. It's never going to produce for you the way it would have produced. And that lack of satisfaction in your work will be a cosmic reminder to you that your relationship with your Creator is broken. You'll feel this whenever you are searching for your purpose and looking for meaning and still are left wanting."

Have you felt that? There are dreams inside you—goals, visions, and hopes of what your life could become—but you just can't seem to live them out. You just can't seem to find that elusive piece that makes life a dream. You feel incapable of making your dreams come to fruition, making them real. Your gut keeps telling you you're missing the life you were created to live. You've missed your destiny. It steals whatever pleasure a moment might have had, because in the end you know something's missing.

Maybe you have accomplished so much and have a résumé five miles long, yet you are dissatisfied with your life. You've given up on the idea that any great accomplishment will ever fulfill you. When we are disenfranchised from God, and our brokenness diminishes our capacity to enjoy even the successes and the relationships in our lives.

But through Jesus, God reverses the curse. You can have a meaningful marriage; you can make lifelong friends; you can open your life to people and build the kind of community you have never known but always longed for. You can get up on Monday morning and actually be glad that you are going to work. You don't have to be a slave to your job. Some of you lack the courage to quit the job you were never supposed to have because you are so afraid that there is no better life out there for you.

When you grow in your relationship with God and allow him to give you his dreams for your life, he gives you the courage to live them out. You will find a purpose so extraordinary that it wakes you up in the morning, and you want to give all you have to make it come to pass.

PURE JOY

James, the brother of Jesus, tells us that when you enjoy life, something else happens to you. You begin to be free of your circumstances. You are released from the environment in which you live, no longer dependent on your surroundings to bring you joy and enjoyment.

James writes, "Dear brothers and sisters, whenever trouble comes your way, let it be an opportunity for joy." Now if I asked you what brought you joy in life, you probably wouldn't think, *Oh that's easy—hardship, trials, and roadblocks to my goals and dreams.* Yet the place of suffering and trial, James tells us, is the very place where joy should be experienced. James is saying that we are no longer dependent on our circumstances to produce pleasure, joy, and enjoyment of life. We can rise above that.

Now there are some days that are given to pleasure, aren't there? You wake up and it's sunny and beautiful, but breezy and cool. You can get a suntan without sweating. You can't even see the smog. Bono was right, it's a beautiful day. You don't remember filling up the car with gas, but your tank is full and your car is clean. It's a good day all around. If you're married, he's the husband you always thought he should have been but usually isn't. But today he is. He kisses you good morning, and there is no morning breath. His hair is perfect—messy but cool. She's ravishing. You look at her and think, *What is the point of makeup on a face like that?* Angels turn away in shame. Thank God she was willing to marry down.

It's one of those days. Even your skinny clothes fit. Traffic? Like the parting of the Red Sea, all the cars move aside, no traffic in your lane. You get to work five minutes late and your boss asks you why you're early . . . then he gives you a promotion.

Life is good. You enjoy it. You love God. God loves you. Life is beautiful. God is everywhere. Beauty is everywhere to behold.

Then you wake up the next day, and it's raining and you forgot to roll your car windows up. You turn on the weather and discover you've just slept through the first monsoon in your region's history. Everything goes downhill from there, and you wonder, *Where is God?* You hate your job and your boss, not to mention your life. You're angry and bitter against God. Life is dragging you around like a piece of toilet paper stuck to the bottom of its shoe.

James calls us to rise above it all. You can't avoid the difficulties of life, but you don't have to be defined by them. While we are in the fray, we can live above the trials, difficulties, and disappointments that would otherwise bring us down. We have become a culture of despair and depression. It seems our only solution is medication.

Recently I saw a commercial hawking a specialized antidepressant. It talked about seasonal affective disorder. I understand there are people who are suffering from it, but I think far too many of us are controlled by whatever season is coming our way. One of the ways to reduce the effects of seasonal affective disorder is to get some light. Maybe we need to stop living in the dark and get in the light. This brings new light to Jesus' words, "I am the light of the world" (John 8:12). Maybe we need to get into the light of Jesus and allow him to infuse some enjoyment into our lives even on the darkest of days.

SACRED PLEASURE

Let's take what James proposes about joy, and then connect the dots with Nehemiah's insights on joy. Nehemiah gives us a mandate to enjoy life. It is perhaps the most sacred invitation you will ever receive. Why do we conclude that the people who are truly spiritual are the ones who are sober, serious, and joyless? Many people think spirituality is a journey toward numbness. Someone once told me, "I see people going into that church all happy and coming out all depressed. I don't want to go there. Isn't it supposed to be the other way around?" No, that's not right either. We're supposed to come in happy too—or at least expectant.

Nehemiah tells of a time when the Scriptures had been lost. His generation had never seen or heard anyone read their Holy Book. They knew the stories. They had the commandments written in their hearts and minds. The traditions had been passed on orally. Though they treasured what was given them by their elders, the Israelites had a vacuum in their faith experience. But finally, the book of God had been found.

Ezra stood on the platform in full view of all the people. When they saw him open the book, they all rose to their feet. Then Ezra praised the LORD, the great God, and all the people chanted, "Amen! Amen!" [Which, by the way, is why I pray, "Amen and amen." People ask me that all the time. It's because of this passage.] as they lifted their hands toward heaven. Then they bowed down and worshiped the LORD with their faces to the ground.

Now the Levites . . . instructed the people who were standing there. They read from the Book of the Law of God and clearly explained the meaning of what was being read, helping the people understand each passage. [Isn't that a phenomenal idea, read the Bible and explain it so it makes sense?] Then Nehemiah the governor, Ezra the priest and scribe, and the Levites who were interpreting for the people said to them, "Don't weep on such a day as this! For today is a sacred day before the LORD your God." All the people had been weeping as they listened to the words of the law.

How the people responded makes perfect sense. They hadn't heard the Word of God for so long. They knew it was a holy moment. Ezra stood up and opened the Scriptures, and the people all rose to their feet and started shouting and raising their hands toward heaven. When they heard the Scriptures explained, they understood who God is and who they were and how short they had fallen short of God's intent for their lives. They threw themselves on the ground and began weeping and weeping and weeping. This is the natural response when we are confronted with the holiness of God: we are overwhelmed by God's beauty and by our brokenness. We are distraught by our inadequacy. This is where we would stay, left to ourselves—on the floor, weeping in our shame, in our guilt. But Nehemiah, Ezra, and the Levites said, "Don't weep on such a day as this!" Why? "For today is a sacred day before the LORD your God."

Then Nehemiah told the people, "Go and celebrate" (v. 10). Can you imagine what it must have been like when they heard this?

If you heard God speak through his Word, go and celebrate life. Nehemiah said, "Go and celebrate with a feast of choice foods and sweet drinks, and share gifts of food with people who have nothing prepared. This is a sacred day before our LORD. Don't be dejected and sad, for the joy of the LORD is your strength!"

The Israelites not only found the lost parchments, but they discovered the principle to finding the strength to create a new and better future. The less you enjoy your life, the weaker you will be on your journey. Why? Because the joy of the Lord is your strength. The strength of the living God becomes your strength when you enjoy God and he enjoys you. You increase in strength when you live in God's pleasure. Nothing can stop you from accomplishing what God has awakened in your soul. Your strength is the *joy* of the Lord—not the truth of the Lord, or the knowledge of the Lord, or even the power of the Lord, but the joy. Your strength is not the rituals, not the religion, not the doctrine, and not the disciplines. The more you enjoy God and enjoy the life he calls you into, the stronger you will be. To enjoy life is a sacred act of worship.

"And the Levites, too, quieted the people, telling them, 'Hush! Don't weep! For this is a sacred day.'" We often think that the most sacred days are the days we're most somber. Vows of silence, acts of contrition, penance—these are the marks of the sacred, right? We think, *It's a sacred day; let's mourn. It's a sacred place; let's be silent.* We know exactly what it means when we are told to be reverent. Be honest: how many of you have taken your kids to church, and when they are talking or laughing, you shush them and tell them, "Be quiet, you're in church." But church should be a place where our children laugh and sing and enjoy the life God gave them. One of the worst things we can do is put someone in a context where he is bored to death in a supposedly sacred moment. No wonder so many people run for their lives when they see Christianity and search for some other path to joy.

"So the people went away to eat and drink at a festive meal, to share gifts of food, and to celebrate with great joy because they had heard God's words and understood them." God is saying that you were created to enjoy life. You were designed for pleasure. There is a reason your spirit naturally gravitates toward laughter and celebration, why it takes fewer muscles to smile than it does to frown. You were physiologically designed to laugh, to play, and to enjoy. And this is your sacred ambition. The world would be as God imagined it if every human being was living a life of joy. We have somehow equated worship with singing, yet the worship leader isn't necessarily the person onstage singing during a church service; it is any person who guides us into a life where we enjoy life best and most.

When we were in seminary, Kim and I had a friend whom I considered the holiest guy in the whole place. There was a reason: he was the most despondent person I knew. I watched this guy and thought, *This is one holy guy. He is always down and dark and brooding.* Me, I was having a good time. I was hanging out with Kim and playing racquetball, enjoying life, having a blast. I would leave on a Friday, be gone for a week, and come back. I traveled all over the country. I had no money, but you can catch a ride almost anywhere.

I'd be around him and think, *I am such a pagan.* I would ask him, "How are you doing today?" He would always say, "The Lord is really breaking me." And I'd think, *Wow, he's really holy; God's almost never breaking me. I wonder what's wrong.* I figured I was a lost cause—there was no point in breaking me any worse than I was already.

Other times I would ask him, "How are you doing today?" And

he would say, "Oh, the Lord is disciplining me." He always seemed to be in deep places with the Father, while I was off playing. This went on for a couple of years. I even thought one time we should plan a conference on holiness and he should teach it. I concluded I didn't know how to get that deep because I couldn't get that down.

One day it came to me. I asked him again, "How are you doing today?" I knew the answer. His heart was heavy. God was breaking him. This time I asked him what he kept doing to set God off. If God was always breaking me, I'd do something to change that. You know, he was a really sincere and devout person, but somewhere down the road someone had taught him that holiness is the absence of happiness.

He represents so many sincere people. I would like to set as many as possible free from that prison of spiritual abuse. Faith isn't supposed to rob your joy but enhance it. God is love. God is life. You cannot know God's love and not enjoy life. This is where you genuinely become the life of the party. Holiness does not leave you hollow, it makes you a hedonist. No one should enjoy life more than you. Paul tells us, "Do not be drunk with wine, but be drunk with the Holy Spirit." Drink up! Drink deep! Enjoy life. Enjoy all the beauty around you. Let each moment be filled with wonder. When God's Spirit comes to us, He awakens the hero within us who finds strength in the joy of God's presence. This hero could be called nothing less than hedonist.

Have you subtly bought in to the belief that holiness is the absence of pleasure, of delight, of desire, of laughter, of joy, of enjoyment? I want you to remember that humanity started in the garden of pleasure with everything leveraged in our direction so we could enjoy God, enjoy each other, and enjoy life. The reason we don't enjoy life is because our souls ate damaged and we need

God to heal us of our wounds. To come to God is to come to joy. To live in God's presence is to know his pleasure. To live in Jesus is to live in joy.

Walk with God, and get ready—it's going to be exhilarating. Life will become a gift. When you dream with your eyes open, even when you shouldn't find joy, even when life comes at you hard, even when you have tremendous pain and disappointment and you have every good reason to lose your joy, deep in the core of your soul there will be an unshakable joy.

When you live an awakened life, all your senses are on alert. You are fully alive and fully able to experience the true pleasure of life. You're an artist, an explorer, an alchemist, a believer, a seer, an activist and a hedonist. You might as well get used to it. Enjoy!

invest

THE ROMANTIC

I WAS SPEAKING AT AN EVENT WHERE I MET OLIVE backstage. Olive Aneno was born in 1979 in a rural village called Kitgum along the volatile northern border of Uganda pressing against Sudan. Olive and her sister, who was blind, would attend school at day then sleep in the bush at night in order to avoid the rebel militia that would capture the villagers' children and force them to become child soldiers. She remembers how at the age of six she awoke one night with a large python circling around her while she laid still and prayed for her life. At the age of twelve she was orphaned by HIV/AIDS which took both her mother and aunt within two weeks of one another and left eight children to survive on their own. During this time she had been enrolled in a child development program through Compassion International, which partnered with a local faith community. It was here that her life intersected with a family from across the world in Australia. Hans and Maria Schroo had four children of their own and as a family sponsored Olive and invested in her future. Against all odds, Olive earned a scholarship into Makerere University in Kampala. Within a year she was offered a full athletic scholarship to South Carolina State University to play volleyball. She not only received her bachelor of science degree but continues on to earn her master's degree in Social Work at the University of Georgia. She has since begun to invest her life in counseling children with mental and emotional disorders as well as working with at-risk children and advocating for children trapped in poverty around the world.

Olive is a powerful reminder that the dream and the future of so many across the world are dependent on the investment and compassion of those more fortunate. But this principle doesn't end here. The reality is that all of us need others to succeed. Every successful life is the expression of the investment of many others. This, if for no other reason, is why people are our most important investment. Success is the result of making wise investments, and there is no wiser investment than investing in people. And by the way, real success *never* happens alone. If you are successful, you should be equally grateful. *All* great lives are the product of the great investment of others. If there is a hero within you that must be awakened it is this one—the one I call the Romantic. This attribute is critical to your future. It will be the difference not only between failure and success, but fulfillment and regret. Learning to invest is a life lesson that brings life. It is perhaps the most essential attribute to creating a life that is bigger than your dreams.

RELATIONAL EQUITY

Kim is always asking me how many jobs I am going to take on. This, I am sure, is related to my admitted struggle with focus. There is another reason, though. There are people in my life I can help who were there for me when I needed help. One of my most longstanding roles is as futurist for Bethel University and Seminary. There are universities all over Los Angeles, but I fly to St. Paul and the East Coast and drive down to their San Diego campus to serve them in any way I can. Even though I'm not even a big fan of seminaries! They already know this. I am, though, a big fan of the people involved and associated with this school. About fifteen years ago, when I was struggling to feed my family and pay the bills, this Swedish community showed up and offered me an opportunity to use my gifts and take care of my family.

It wasn't a job they offered; it was a relationship. The job was so elusive it was impossible to quantify. It was an invitation to make a contribution not based on a role but based on their belief that I had something unique to offer. For some reason they just believed in me—they chose to invest in who I was and what God might do through my life. In my mind, you don't work for a company or an organization; you work with people—who join together to fulfill a common mission.

I also serve on a board for an organization called Vision 360. They are committed to the huge goal of starting communities of faith in cities all over the world. I serve there because Steve Johnson asked me to. One weekend fifteen years ago, Steve and his brother, Doug, and a third team member named Dave Olsen invited me to join them in their insane and exhilarating projects. Work had rarely been so much fun. They are some of the most caring and loyal people I have ever known. I am there with them because they were there with me. I hope fifteen years from now, our relationship will have been mutually beneficial. All of these relationships are interconnected. We started small with great dreams and committ-ment to each other. Nearly twenty years later we have shared over and over in each others' success.

I've been told that my weakness is that I'm too loyal—I can live with that. Time has taught me that relational investment is more than worth the risk. It's perplexing to me that people can be more committed to their financial investments than what they invest in people. The people you invest in now are the people who will be invested in you tomorrow. And if you live as if you don't need people, you will get to prove it later.

MOVE FAST, BUT WALK SLOWLY

It might be surprising, but even in Los Angeles you run into a lot of senior adults. Occasionally, you meet someone whose life has been so admirable you marvel at how he or she has lived so well. Often you meet a lot of lonely older people. At first you assume they have just outlived their family and friends. But as you get to know them, you realize that's not usually the case. Their family is alive, but not well. Their children are estranged from them. They have few, if any, friends. My wife, Kim, who has an endless supply of compassion for those she meets, often ends up filling the space their families have left vacant. When you hear these lonely seniors tell their stories, you realize they were not there for their kids, and now their kids are not there for them.

There is a stark reality with which I have come face to face, one each of us needs to embrace before it is too late. The people you make time for will find time for you.

When my son, Aaron, was a little guy, he would often struggle behind me, trying to keep up. I would get focused on something and not even realize how fast I was walking. When Aaron couldn't go any faster, he would plead, "Daddy, wait up!"

One day it hit me: he will only know what I teach him. I stopped and knelt down so we could talk face-to-face, man-to-man. I said, "Buddy, I'm sorry. I promise I will slow down and wait for you. And when I'm old and you're strong, I want you to remember that I waited for you. I want you to slow down and walk with me then. Okay?" I don't know how much of that he understood, but the lesson was good for me anyway. Now that he is his own man at twenty we still love working together.

Take time to invest in the people who are in your life. Slow down if you have to, and bring them with you. It is better to adjust your pace than to walk alone. A life well lived isn't about who walks the fastest but about who has the most people walking with them. You can't make time for everyone, but you can make time for someone. So invest well.

Jesus himself makes this point through perhaps his most unusual and perplexing parable—a story about a guy who is less than admirable and finishes ahead.

There was a rich man whose manager was accused of wasting his possessions.

So he called him in and asked him, "What is this I hear about you? Give an account of your management, because you cannot be manager any longer."

The manager said to himself, "What shall I do now? My master is taking away my job. I'm not strong enough to dig, and I'm ashamed to beg—I know what I'll do so that, when I lose my job here, people will welcome me into their houses."

So he called in each one of his master's debtors. He asked the first, "How much do you owe my master?"

"Nine hundred gallons of olive oil," he replied.

The manager told him, "Take your bill, sit down quickly, and make it four hundred and fifty."

Then he asked the second, "And how much do you owe?"

"A thousand bushels of wheat," he replied.

He told him, "Take your bill and make it eight hundred."

So far there's really nothing redeeming in this parable. You have a bad manager who gets fired, so he starts forgiving the debt of his master's debtors so that later on he might have someone who will like him enough to help him out. Now you expect this is where Jesus would rebuke us or call us to a higher standard. The point, you think, would be, don't be like that bad manager.

Jesus continues, "The master commended the dishonest manager because he had acted shrewdly." Wait a minute—Jesus is actually highlighting this guy as an example! He was a corrupt manager who misappropriated funds that were not his, but the master commended him for being shrewd. And Jesus, the paragon of integrity, is telling us the crook in the parable is smarter than those of us who are striving to live lives of integrity.

Jesus says, "For the people of this world are more shrewd in dealing with their own kind than are the people of the light" (v. 8 TNIV). That's encouraging, isn't it? He goes on. "I tell you, use worldly wealth to gain friends for yourselves so that when it is gone you will be welcomed into eternal dwellings."

Strangely enough, it is here that we find the last but most important attribute of people who live to see their dreams become reality. They invest in people.

THE GREAT INVESTORS

When you read the title of this chapter—"Invest"—did you conclude right away that it would be about money? I figured this would likely be the immediate assumption. What we will discover in this chapter affects our money, but that's not primarily what I'm talking about. And it's not what Jesus is talking about in this parable.

Jesus does emphasize that you need to invest your financial resources well. The point of the parable isn't that you should misdirect other people's money; it's that you should carefully invest your life. We have used our resources well when we have invested in others. Whatever you gain in this world, whatever you accumulate in this life, you need to invest in people. If you don't invest and build into others, your life will not have eternal value.

Jesus commends a guy who is in real trouble. This manager is wrongly motivated. He's getting fired from his job and has no one who will look after him, no one he can turn to. He has not made others a priority in his life. No one cares about him, his problems, his future, or his success. He recognizes the emptiness of his life and the shallowness of his relationships, so he starts forgiving people who owed his master money. His motives are clear: he does this so they might actually like him and feel as if they should do something kind for him later.

The manager's actions in this story are dishonorable, except that he stumbled on a very important principle: there's nothing more important than to invest your life in people. If you do not develop relationships with people who care about your success, you will not achieve the greatness that God desires for you to accomplish. You will not create the life of your dreams without the help of other people. This is not something that we can do alone.

I began noticing this early in my life. From a very early age, I had dreams and ambitions that I lacked the talent and skills to accomplish. I had to decide whether it was more important for that dream to become reality. I knew even then the dream was more important than my success. I could choose lesser dreams, goals, and ambitions, or I would have to admit my inability to succeed alone and acknowledge my need for others. I began developing the skills needed to build teams that could accomplish together what I could never even dream of making happen alone.

If I caught on to this early, it's only because I had a distinct advantage. I was never great at anything. Some people have the liability of great talent. They are protégés who stand out and above the crowd. They can do so much without anyone else's help. Yet these people don't have to learn the skills of diplomacy and defer facing the crisis of their own inadequacy. I only know this from observation, because I had to face this very early in my life. What do you do when you have great dreams and inadequate talent? You have to believe in the greatness of others.

Now the dilemma is this: you might keep trying to recruit proven talent to advance your dreams, but they have their own dreams and only want to work with proven talent—so you don't qualify. It's like a catch-22. You can't make it happen until you get the talent, and you can't get the talent until you make it happen. What do you do? Well at least two things. One, you give yourself to making the dreams of others a reality. Two, you see everyone as pre-great. Your job becomes to help others succeed and to develop their God-given potential.

When your potential is limited by who you are, of course you have limitations. When your potential is measured by whom you serve, your potential is unlimited. This applies in relation to God and to people. When you live your life serving God and others, the sky is the limit. You can complain that your dreams are bigger than your capacity, or you can see this as proof that the dream God has placed on your heart has room for more people than just you.

I grappled with this when I began to feel that the world was unfair not only in the distribution of talent but also in the distribution of grace. I noticed that some people seem to receive a disproportionate amount of grace. Many times in my life, I have failed, and I've seen someone else fail. But somehow I was able to work my way through that failure, while the other person could not. This is not because I was stronger; in fact, often I seemed weaker. I've made mistakes and have been embraced with forgiveness, while others made similar mistakes and did not find any consolation.

Have you ever noticed that two people can commit the same offense and not be treated the same way? There is supposed to be justice and fairness in the world, and especially in the church, but that's not always true. You might blow it big-time, take on a huge endeavor and absolutely mess up, yet somehow you come out of that rubble, and people entrust you with other responsibilities and more resources. It's almost as if you never failed at all. Or you might have a much less significant failure but can't seem to recover from it. You look at the first person and wonder, *Wait a minute. He blew it bigger than me, and he got another chance. What's the deal? I had a small failure, just a small infraction, and I can't find the level of grace and investment in me to help me overcome it.*

Sometimes it's about talent. Organizations that are focused on success and not character often overlook moral failure in their talent. Ironically, though, if these people don't produce, they are tossed out like day-old garbage. Yet there are individuals who can fail in a huge endeavor and still not lose their value to the organization. I've watched this over time. I've seen people who did not have enough emotional and relational reserve to help them overcome their failures. They hold their jobs by a thread. One messup, one misstep, and they're gone. They have no relational net to catch them when they fall or fail. These people constantly feel as if others are just watching and waiting for them to stumble.

Success can create an illusion or distortion of reality that most leaders don't care to dispel. Throughout my life, I have experienced failure after failure after failure. Yet when I look back, I realize those failures have not defined me. Though I have had fewer successes than failures, I am thankfully marked more by the success than the failure.

I began realizing something in retrospect—there were people around me who refused to let me fail. I can't explain it; it just started happening. There were times I wanted to give up, times I was filled with fear, times I was overwhelmed with doubt, and times I felt paralyzed. There have been times when I was exhausted and did not think I could keep going, and times that I, in my own mind, had already given up. I was overwhelmed with a sense of failure. I realize now that during these times, other people refused to leave me there. They picked me up, dusted me off, pointed me in the right direction, and somehow got me back on track.

LOVE THEM OR LEAVE THEM

Sadly, that isn't true for everyone. Why do some people get the benefit of help from others and others do not? Nearly a decade ago, when I wrote my first book, *An Unstoppable Force*, I penned this acknowledgment in the opening statement: "My failures are my gift to others and my successes are the gift of others to me."

If you neglect the importance of building healthy relationships, you will find yourself alone in the midst of crisis. When you invest in others, they will leverage even your failures to be the material for your future success. What I began to experience in the most wonderful way is that when you live in healthy community, others count it their success when you succeed. I am absolutely convinced that you will never create the life of your dreams until you make people your highest value. Invest your life in people, and you will begin to build for yourself a relational net that catches you when you fall and picks you up when you're no longer strong enough to walk by yourself. You were never meant to walk alone.

If you live a life of self-importance, you won't find many people who want to help you when your life starts falling apart. If you can move yourself out of the center and begin to give your life away to other people, you'll begin to find that those very people will rally around you when you need them the most. We have to make a personal commitment that our goals, ambitions, and dreams will never overtake our value for people.

We must change from relational consumers and become investors. We don't say it like this, but far too many see people as just another commodity—another resource. Do you see people as something to be used for your benefit, to accomplish your goals, to help you achieve your success, and then to be disposed of? Or do you see people as a gift and a stewardship? Are you motivated by selfish ambition or by unconditional love?

A business book by Tim Sanders is a great reminder of this value. The book is called *Love Is the Killer App*, and its premise is simple: if you want the killer application to take your company to the next level, here it is—it's love. If you could just learn to invest in people and build relationships and value community and be truly human, it could change everything.

Sanders followed that book with another one with a similar theme, titled *The Likeability Factor*. Again Sanders captures something all of us need to consider. He points out some things that are kind of obvious. The people we elect to positions tend to be people who are likable. In fact, one characteristic common among all the US presidents is that people considered them likable—at least before they became commander in chief. Students who are considered likable by teachers get better grades, and teachers who are considered likable by students get better reviews. Employees who are likable while doing the same level and quality of work as other employees who are not as likable get better reviews. The truth of the matter is that likable people tend to get more promotions, more breaks, more understanding, more empathy, more compassion, and, yes, even more forgiveness.

In these two books, Sanders focuses on relational themes: friendliness, your ability to communicate liking and openness to others; relevance, your capacity to connect with others' interests, wants, and needs; empathy, your ability to recognize, acknowledge, and experience other people's feelings; and realness, the integrity that stands behind your likability and guarantees your authenticity.

Has it ever occurred to you that the dreams that God created you to live are things you cannot accomplish or achieve alone? God never intended for you or me to live our lives in isolation. Great dreams always have room for the greatness of others. Great leaders are not diminished by the greatness of others. The world will only get better when we start valuing and investing in one another.

When I came home from a recent trip to Australia and New Zealand, I hadn't seen any American television in a while, so I went to my trusty TiVo and downloaded some meaningless entertainment. I had the closing episode of *The Apprentice* waiting for me. One year, one of the teams was called Mosaic, and that added a little more incentive to become a fan. This particular year, the contestants were divided into two teams—street smarts versus book smarts. One group consistent of players who had been to college; the other team included players who had not been to college. The series played out fairly evenly that year. Formal education didn't seem to make a difference. It only mattered that they were smart.

The final two contestants were a book-smart person versus a street-smart person. Each contestant was given an assignment and a team. Of course, to make good television, each leader's team consisted of the three people she liked the least. So the book-smart person was given the three people that, if you watched the show, you would say were sort of like idiot savants. They were really bright people who had no clue about life. That's who the book-smart Kendra got.

Tana got the three people who were street-smart. All of them were extraordinarily aggressive, angry, intense, and of course, hard to work with.

Each team had a business-oriented task, but the real challenge was for the contestants to learn how to work with people they didn't like. How do you rally a team of people who don't like you? The process was a fascinating experiment in human relationships.

Kendra, to the surprise of everyone, won such devotion among her three colleagues, who had not really respected each other highly before. She treated them with respect, and they in turn treated her with respect. They performed exceptionally well. Her team members performed better for her than they did even for themselves. When their task was over, they hugged and cried and actually had a sense of loss when they had to go their own ways.

Tana, on the other hand, continually demeaned her team. She called them the Three Stooges and berated them, making jokes at their expense. As I watched the show, I kept wondering, *How can a person be this successful in life and act like this on television?* Everything is being recorded for millions to see—not to mention your teammates, when the segment finally airs. What you discover is you can't hide your core—who you really are—when you're being watched all the time.

Tana treated her team like they were her servants. Because she considered them stupid and of no value, they performed at a lower level than they could have. They became for her who she saw them to be. Her team lived down to her expectations. Even when her three colleagues were performing well, she had so little trust in them that she kept micromanaging them. When the task was over, it became clear that the real challenge was the way she related to her team. Even when Tana waved good-bye, she did so in a condescending way, as if she was better than the others.

Here were two people who would be considered high achievers, Kendra and Tana, and yet the defining factor in their success in this task was how they treated others. How about you? Do you treat people as the most valuable resource in your organization—in your life?

Who Will Carry You?

The Bible describes an event in the life of Jesus that accentuates the importance of committing our lives to investing in others.

A few days later, when Jesus again entered Capernaum, the people heard that he had come home. So many gathered that there was no room left, not even outside the door, and he preached the word to them. Some men came bringing to him a paralytic, carried by four of them. Since they could not get him to Jesus because of the crowd, they made an opening in the roof above Jesus and, after digging through it, lowered the mat the paralyzed man was lying on. When Jesus saw their faith, he said to the paralytic, "Son, your sins are forgiven."

Now some teachers of the law were sitting there, thinking to themselves, "Why does this fellow talk like that? He's blaspheming! Who can forgive sins but God alone?"

Immediately Jesus knew in his Spirit that this was what they were thinking in their hearts, and he said to them, "Why are you thinking these things? Which is easier: to say to the paralytic, 'Your sins are forgiven,' or to say, 'Get up, take your mat and walk'? But that you may know that the Son of Man has authority on earth to forgive sins. . . ." He said to the paralytic, "I tell you, get up, take your mat and go home." He got up, took his mat and walked out in full view of them all. This amazed everyone and they praised God, saying, "We have never seen anything like this!"

Now, of course, the main point in documenting this particular experience is to confirm that Jesus Christ is God. The Israelites understood that only God had the power to forgive sins. So when Jesus told the man, "Your sins are forgiven," they considered it blasphemy because that's something only God can do. So Jesus pressed them and said, "Is it easier to say your sins are forgiven or to take up your mat and walk?" I love how Jesus' questions are more powerful than our answers.

It's easier to say your sins are forgiven, isn't it? Especially when you're looking at a paralytic. I mean the chances of a paralytic standing to his feet when you say, "Get up and walk" are really low if you're not God. But you might say, "Your sins are forgiven," and no one will really know. The person might actually feel better. When Jesus asked which one is easier, it was a trick question. Of course it's easier to say your sins are forgiven; so when he told the paralytic, "Take up your mat and walk," and the guy was healed, it forced everyone to face the prospect that Jesus was God walking among them.

It's easy to miss, but there's something else going on in this story that relates to our topic. There is a guy who is paralyzed. He needed to get to Jesus and couldn't because he was paralyzed. But he did have four loyal, committed, and inventive friends who picked up the four corners of his mat and carried him to Jesus. There were so many people listening to Jesus that they couldn't get to him. Failure was clearly not an option, so eventually they found a way. It was destructive, but they did it anyway. They climbed on top of the house and cut a hole in the roof. Aren't these guys creative? They are out-of-the-box thinkers. They opened a hole in the roof and carefully dropped their friend at the feet of Jesus—cutting a hole and cutting in line.

Have you ever gotten mad at the driver who speeds past you and cuts in front of you on the exit ramp? You would have absolutely hated these guys. If you were sitting outside the house trying to listen to Jesus and all of a sudden you see the roof opening up and some vandals cutting in line in front of you, you would have been ticked. It's important to note that Jesus did not send these men to the back of the line, by the way. Their creative approach actually got Jesus' attention.

Now something strange happens. When they dropped their friend in front of Jesus, the Bible says this: "When Jesus saw their faith, he said to the paralytic, 'Son, your sins are forgiven'" (v. 2 NIV).

Now I know everything in the Bible is supposed to make sense, but this doesn't make sense. If the Bible said, "When Jesus saw *the paralytic's* faith, he said to him, 'Son, your sins are forgiven,'" that would make sense. But the verse says, "When Jesus saw *their* faith"—the faith of the man's friends. That doesn't make any sense, does it? It's like you putting in your ATM card and entering your PIN number, punching in the numbers for five hundred dollars, and the person in the next ATM getting the money. It doesn't make any sense. After all, isn't the forgiveness of sins a very personal thing? You can't get your sins forgiven because someone else has faith, can you? That seems totally out of line with everything we understand from the Scriptures.

Or is it possible that we have such a Western, individualistic view of our spirituality that we can't see things from God's vantage point? God does not measure our individual spirituality by looking at us isolated from the people in our lives. God measures our spiritual health or spiritual dysfunction by the relationships and community and the people around us.

When Jesus saw the commitment these four men had for their friend, he forgave the paralytic's sins. Maybe God knows more about us by the people who know us than by what we know about ourselves. On account of the faith of these four loyal friends, Jesus said to the paralytic, "Your sins are forgiven."

There's something else going on here. These four guys cut in line, climbed a roof, vandalized a home, and dropped their friend at the feet of Jesus, yet there seems to be no personal benefit for them. Consider this: if God saw your faith, wouldn't you want something out of it? I mean if Jesus saw your faith, wouldn't you want him to say, "Your property value is going to double"? Or "You're going to get a promotion at work"? Or "Tomorrow you'll be better looking; go in peace"? If you have faith, shouldn't it be personally beneficial? A lot of the faith talk today is about how to get a better life for you. We want our faith to have benefits that are nontransferable—like all our important memberships and benefits.

So the guy on the mat is healed from his paralysis. All the benefit goes to the one person whose faith is not worth noting, and none of the benefit goes to the four men whom Jesus said had faith. Do you really think the friends left disappointed? They had moved to the level of living that they found satisfaction in the healing and wholeness of their friend. His success was their success.

Do you have friends you refuse to leave behind? As you pursue your dreams and goals and ambitions, do you have people in your life who are the kind of friends that, if they were not with you, you could no longer define that endeavor as successful? We all need the kind of friends we can turn to and say, "Even if I have to pick up your mat and carry you with me, I will not go any farther on this journey without you." We all need people we are invested in, friends we give our life to no matter what may come, people who matter more to us than ourselves.

When a man and woman walk an aisle and say, "Till death do us part," I imagine they are profoundly sincere. I don't think any of them ever imagines in that moment that everything could one day change. As time goes by, no one consciously decides, "From this point forward, I'm going to stop loving my spouse." When you end up in divorce, it's probably not because you made a conscious decision to devalue your spouse. It's more likely because you had a subconscious focus on your goals and ambitions, and you kept pushing the value of that person further and further down the list. No one says, "In twenty years, I want to be a stranger to you. In fifteen years, I don't want you to be able to remember why you loved me." No one plans the loss of love. You have to plan to preserve it. There are far too many people who have lost the one they loved simply because their highest value was not love.

Is there someone you refuse to leave behind? I'm absolutely

certain there isn't a mother who tenderly cares for and nurtures a child, and thinks, *I hope in twenty years this child despises me and never gives me a call.* I don't think there's a father, as cold and callous as he may look on the outside, who holds his newborn son or daughter and thinks, *I hope one day this person is my closest enemy.* But I meet parents all the time who are desperately trying to establish a friendship with their child. But the problem is that their child is now grown and living on the other coast. The time to build a lifelong friendship with your child is long before they have their own children. If you are a stranger to your family, do not be surprised when you find yourself estranged.

Many times in life, all the things of lesser importance crowd people out of the center. We soon find ourselves isolated and alone.

All for One for All

There was no reason for those four guys to work their way over the crowd onto that roof, cut open a hole, and lower their friend before Jesus except that this paralytic mattered to them.

So here's the million-dollar question: do you have friends who value you so highly because of the investment you've made in their lives that they wouldn't leave you behind? If you were paralyzed, if the place you needed to go to fulfill your dreams you could not get to alone, if what you needed to do you could not accomplish alone, do you have at least four people in your life who care enough about you to not leave you behind? Most of us would be hard-pressed to think of four people who have a deep and meaningful commitment to us.

In this particular story, we find five people who are committed to one another at a level that impressed God. One, even though paralyzed, somehow gained the affection of the other four, who were willing to risk and sacrifice for his sake.

So let me ask you again, are there people in your life you refuse to leave behind? Are there people you will not allow yourself to define success without? Are there people you've so invested in and built such a strong relationship with that you know when you struggle and when you fall, when you are weak, when you doubt, that they'll come and get you?

If you don't invest in people, they're not going to invest in you. If you don't make people your highest value, eventually the grace of even the best people runs out. In the end people will invest in people who invest in others. I still meet people who walk into churches longing for community and walk out without finding it. It's not always because of a defect in the church. Sometimes it's because we have lost the ability to build relationships.

Jesus says we need to be at least as wise as those who are shrewd in this world. We need to look at our resources. He tells us to take our earthly wealth and invest it in people. Invest it in building friendships. He's not saying that we should try to buy people's love, but he is saying that we should make people more important than all the stuff we have. Use whatever you have been given, whatever you gain, for the service of others, and when it's all gone and you leave this world, you'll receive a great welcome in eternity.

Four friends helped one friend get to Jesus. The real measure of our lives will not be all the things we obtain or all the goals we achieve or all the successes we acquire. Real success will be the relationships we have built, the lives we have touched, the people we have loved and who have loved us and invested in us.

When you live an awakened life, you become a shrewd investor. You believe the future is in people. This is where God has taught you to place your value. All the resources you need to live out the greatness of your dreams are in the people whose lives you touch. They are your legacy. You believe in the power of love and are willing to take the risks of living in the thick of human community. You know we all fail each other. For you, though, there is no other way. You are a romantic at your core, and the romantic is the hero within you waiting to be awakened. Your life, success, and values are all connected to relationships. It's all about people.

If this is not yet who you are, I want to assure you of one thing: you can achieve success and be alone, but you cannot achieve success alone. It's impossible to experience sustainable, enjoyable success alone. If you will invest your life in people, giving others your time, your energy, your attention, your kindness, your compassion, and your forgiveness, if you'll start giving yourself away to others, then you will find in your weakest moments that there are people around you who will refuse to allow you to fail. They will pick you up, lift you up, drag you forward, carry you in, and get you across the finish line so you will fulfill the dream God has placed in your heart.

When you dream with your eyes open, what you see is people. Maybe you were asleep but now you are wide awake, and it's time to dream for others until everyone has a dream worth living for. When you live wide awake you dream, discover, adapt, expect, focus, create, enjoy, and invest. And what you invest in others is all you have become on the journey. You have lived your life giving your life away. You choose to journey with others even when walking alone would have been easier and less complicated. Now you bask in the gift of friendship and community. You are the romantic and without hesitation or regret you have lived a life of love.

imagine

THE HUMAN

As I mentioned in chapter 1, I spent several weeks working in Africa, culminating with a conference for global entrepreneurs in Arusha, Tanzania. This event was a convergence of some of the brightest minds and courageous spirits the African continent (or this planet, for that matter) has ever known.

I knew somehow this book would be linked to my African experience, but I could have never fully understood how. The problems of Africa are daunting. It would be easy to become so overwhelmed by the immensity of the crisis that we simply lose our resolve and surrender to the realization that we are only human. We could even frame our retreat as an act of faith by declaring that problems this big can only be left to God. At first I was uncertain about writing this book. It could so easily become a formula for self-indulgence. Yet it was here, in Africa, that the connection became clear.

It is my deepest conviction that what humanity ultimately needs is to connect to its Creator. I have come to know the path I have shared with you in these pages only because of Jesus and his grace toward me. It is this grace—in its full measure—I hope you come to know.

Africa became for me a clarion call. A life that awakens the heroic in all of us is not supplemental, but essential. Africa cannot be fixed; it must be re-created. Not by us who have even the most noble of intentions, but by her own heroes. We must serve them and make their journey less perilous where possible—and more possible where impossible. It is they who must reimagine Africa and lead in her re-creation, but it all begins with a dream. As I have said before, you cannot do everything you dream (no matter what Disney tells you), but you cannot do anything until you dream. For us to create a better world together and usher in a more beautiful future, we must awaken the heroic imagination within us all.

I was struck by how many young African leaders were actually against foreign aid. Some went as far as to say that foreign aid was crippling the future of the continent they love. Bono, who has given his passion and influence to create a better future for the masses in poverty, reminded us that aid has been a great help to his native Ireland. He wanted the African leaders to know there is no shame in receiving outside help.

What struck me was not the argument concerning foreign aid, but that the individuals who were really making a difference in the most difficult of situations were the ones who had great dreams and the courage to pursue them. Among those who spoke there was one whose words struck me as both profound and hopeful. I believe his name was Ken Ofori-Attah. He is the founder of Databank in Ghana. Having left his job on Wall Street, he moved back to his native Ghana in 1990 and founded the country's first investment bank. He said, "We the willing have been doing so much with so little for so long, we can now do anything with nothing."

I've seen how poverty can create a famine of the soul. Dreams become a luxury when your sleep is filled with the pangs of hunger. I have also seen how having can be the enemy of imagining. The more you have, the more you have to lose. The longer you have, the more you become dependent on the available resources. Wealth often moves us to depending on resources where once we were depending on resourcefulness. If we are not careful, what we have can establish the limitations of what we imagine.

We must resist this at all costs. The Hebrews saw humans as both image and imagination. Created in God's image ("in his image and likeness he created them") we are to reflect his character (Gen. 1:27). Created out of God's imagination ("before you were born I knew you") we are to reflect his creativity (Jer. 1:5). Neither can be done well without him.

CITIZENS OF AN IMAGINE NATION

It was a cold January evening when I found myself in a debate at Columbia University. Seated to my left were two of the most respected minds in higher education. They had so many letters behind their names it would have been impossible for them to have business cards. I felt so uneducated. I felt like saying, "I'm not a doctor, but I play one on TV." No one could appreciate the irony of debating some of the greatest PhDs of any Ivy League university more than me. Our topic for discussion was "what can be known."

There was a scientist, a philosopher, and scapegoat—I was the resident goat. One of the speakers was Dr. Stuart Gill, a graduate of Melbourne University, Australia, who also earned a PhD from Swinburne University. His research focuses on the first billion years of the universe's evolution. He served as a Columbia Science fellow in the department of astronomy. Next to him was Patricia Kitcher, the Mark van Doren professor of humanities. She was a graduate of Wellesley with a PhD from Princeton. She specialized in the psychology of Freud and the philosophy of Kant.

When asked what can be known, Stuart Gill explained that science is limited to empirical evidence. What can be known is what can be proved. When Patricia Kitcher addressed the question, she responded from a philosophical construct built around ethics. What can be known are human actions. Both speakers were extremely thoughtful and persuasive.

When it was my turn to speak, I confessed that I am more an expert on ignorance than on knowledge. As a person of faith, I stand in an awkward position: I know something I'm not supposed to know. Much like Peter when Jesus asked, "Who do you say I am?" Peter responded, "You are the Christ, the Son of the living God." Then Jesus told him, "This was not revealed to you by man, but by my Father in heaven." In other words, "Peter, you cheated."

Eventually the event at Columbia moved to Q&A. The first question came to me. "When you were a child, you had imaginary friends. When you grew up, you gave them up. Why, then, did you keep God?" What a great question. I wasn't expecting that question. That was an Ivy League question if I ever heard one. I began my search for a profound answer. Unfortunately, that search was out loud and in front of an audience.

I began, "First of all, anyone who knows me knows I still haven't given up my imaginary friends. But you're right: when I was a child, I believed in Santa Claus and the Easter Bunny and the Tooth Fairy and the giant rabbit that used to hide in my closet and come out at three in the morning."

By the way, as you might have noticed, some of our imaginary friends come as a part of cultural stories passed on to us, and others come from late nights when we cannot sleep, our rooms are dark, and our imaginations are left to run wild. In either case, as children our beliefs share space with our own creations. Except that those who reinforce our beliefs are the ones we look to for guidance and trust as credible sources of truth. This is at least in part why as children we believe with such great conviction. Truth and mythology are not yet distinguishable. You just can't tell a five-year-old there is nothing under the bed, even when you check yourself. They find you wanting in your ability to perceive reality. Even our beliefs are reinforced by our imaginations.

I think this was the point of the question. "Why did you keep God when you discovered so many of your beliefs were simply products of lies you were told? Isn't God simply something you were led to imagine?" Though God, and Santa Claus for that matter, were not the direct products of my imagination, this is how the question was posed. So I ran with it, and it went something like this.

"I did have imaginary friends that I later grew out of and gave up. I would say, though, that if you have an imaginary friend who changes your life for the better, an imaginary friend who makes you more compassionate and caring, and this friend moves you from a self-centered life to a life that is selfless and sacrificial, then keep that friend because he will be the best friend you will ever have."

Later in my closing remarks, I came back to this question and added that when my son, Aaron, was little, he wouldn't eat his vegetables, but he would go in the backyard and eat dirt. No matter what we did, we couldn't figure out how to reverse his eating preference. I finally told Kim, "Why don't we just throw the food in the backyard and let him go play?" She didn't go for it. But we didn't stop him from eating because he couldn't distinguish between broccoli and rocks. We helped him come to the place where he realized the stuff on the plate was really good for him, while the rocks were pretty hard to digest.

Stay with me: it's going to make sense in a minute—or at least that's the plan.

Aaron also had a vivid imagination. And like eating, we knew he needed to keep imagining. For your body to be healthy, you have to keep eating. For your soul to stay healthy, you have to keep dreaming. Your imagination is the only attribute you share with God. You have no boundaries in your imagination. It is the only place where you have no limitations. You can become someone you have never been. You can go places you have never seen. You can experience a life you have never lived. Is it possible that your imagination is the playground where you and God are to commune and dream together?

If there were a God, it would make perfect sense that we would be able to imagine. When God thinks, it is a creative act. When we allow God into our thoughts, we join him in the creative process. We work so hard at being creators defined by reason, yet we live in a world created by dreamers. The highest act of human intelligence isn't memorizing facts but imagining a new future. Knowledge isn't nearly as important as imagination.

The Divine Playground

Aaron was in fourth grade when his teacher approached me for an informal parent-teacher conference. Aaron, he explained, was talking too much in class. I suggested that the teacher move him away from his friends. "I've tried that. He still kept talking." I then suggested he isolate Aaron and make him sit alone. "I did that too. It didn't help."

Exasperated, he explained, "Mr. McManus, your son keeps talking to himself. He even stood up in the middle of my lecture having a conversation with imaginary friends off who knows where. You've got to tell him to stop daydreaming and start paying attention."

I realized that the world in Aaron's head was more interesting than the world around him. I was actually encouraged that Aaron had such a vivid imagination. I never told him to stop dreaming, but I did ask him to try to pay attention. This wasn't exactly what I meant when I said we should dream wide awake.

I didn't want Aaron to stop living in his imaginary world; I wanted to help him bring his imaginary world to life. Just like eating, it is about learning how to discriminate. When you were a child, using your imagination was second nature. No, that's almost right—it *is* our nature!

You were created to live a life beyond your wildest imagination. This, of course, is quite a prospect when you consider the vastness of the human imagination. You can imagine far more than you will ever live, but you won't live far more than you imagine. To imagine costs you nothing. Not to imagine could cost you everything. To live a life that moves dreams into reality—that's where the real risk comes in. Imagination is adventure without risk. Your imagination is a playground that is for more than child's play. It is the art house where we begin to create the lives we will live.

Who you are flows from what's going on in your head. Your imagination is the place where God begins to create your future. It all starts in your head before you begin heading anywhere. Proverbs 23:7 tells us that as we think in our heart, so we are. Solomon is telling us that what we think is who we are—and who we are becoming.

The things that run around in your imagination actually shape who you are. When we are young, we dream, we imagine, we are boundless in our exploration, in our thoughts and ideas. As others begin to inform our imaginations, an image of who we are and who we can become begins to form—sometimes positively and sometimes negatively. The people you love, respect, and admire the most have a tremendous impact on the boundaries established in your imagination. Especially the affirmation of those whose love, respect, and admiration you spend your life trying to obtain.

Sometimes this can be very destructive. When you hear yourself defined by demeaning language, like "You're stupid," and "You're worthless," those words begin to shape your understanding, your self-worth, and your perception of who you are. That playground known as your imagination becomes more like a junkyard filled with shrapnel, an alley of broken pieces with jagged edges of pain, discouragement, and disappointment.

You may have in your imagination a story that says you will never accomplish anything meaningful and you'll never become anything significant. You may struggle with esteem and your sense of self. You look at other people and see how they can accomplish something spectacular in life, but you are blind to the possibilities in your own life.

If you are what you think, then who are you? Where you go in your imagination is very much who you are going to become. As you dream and as you imagine your life, you either expand the boundaries of who you can become or you establish paralyzing boundaries that constrict and press against you, limiting and narrowing the person you will become.

Do you need to rethink who you are and who you will become? Maybe you need a fresh vision or a new voice in your life telling you who you really are—the gifts and talents, intelligence, and passions, the potential, the undiscovered uniqueness waiting dormant within you. The only One who knows this fully is the One who created you. The One who created you is the One who longs to awaken you. Your thoughts, your dreams, and the boldness of your imagination are defining you today and shaping who you will become tomorrow. Those thoughts and dreams are informed and influenced by the voices in our lives. It is God and God alone who sees your life without limits. Only he sees who you were created to become. Only he knows the real potential of your life. Wouldn't you want the person who believes the most in you and sees the most in you to be the primary informer of your imagination?

DARK IMAGES

We don't need Jesus simply for our life after death; we need him to live this life on earth. Asaph was a psalmist who had great insight on the human condition. In Psalm 73, he says of his own journey, "God you know me. You know I have tried to keep my heart pure." Then he begins to write this assessment of those who pretended to love God but actually mock God. Then Asaph confesses his internal conflict, "Everyone who seems to turn from you, God, is having the life I want to have." He writes, "This is what the wicked are like—always carefree."

Have you ever been envious of people who were living a life you didn't want to live, but you wanted to have the results they had? "God, here I am trying to live for you, and she gets the promotion." Or, "I do the right thing, but he gets the girl." It can be so irritating when you feel like you can't create the life of your dreams, especially when you are trying to do things the right way.

Asaph's language is colorful and dramatic as he describes those he both envies and despises. He says, "Their eye bulges from fatness." What a great way of describing their insatiable appetite for self-indulgent and destructive vices. They consume and devour everything they want. They don't care about how it hurts other people; they just take and take and take.

Then he says, "The imaginations of their heart run riot."

Their imagination has become a very dark and dangerous place. They go to sinister and corrupt places in their minds then flesh out their darkest scenarios in real life. Their dreams become the way they live and the way they treat other people.

Our imagination is a gift from God to us, but it can become a curse. Your dreams, your values, and your passions inform your imagination. When your heart is dead, your imagination creates territories that are dark and destructive. They will corrupt you from the inside out until you become a person you could have never imagined you would be. In this condition, your dreams become a nightmare.

Someone doesn't walk into a high school and kill nearly three dozen people without imagining it first. I assure you the assassin played out the scenario over and over and over again. If you allow your imagination to create territories filled with anger, hatred, bitterness, jealousy, and envy, don't be surprised when one day you discover you've become someone you could not imagine.

A husband doesn't just go off and commit adultery one day. It's not something he had never considered and then, suddenly, one day he is unfaithful. What happens is his imagination went to places he should never have gone, and there it began to shape who he was from the inside until it escaped and became who he was on the outside.

You don't just embezzle ten thousand dollars because, well, it was right there and you had the opportunity. What happened was that your imagination went to overwhelmingly greedy places, and you wanted and wanted and wanted and it was never enough, and you had to have more than you could actually afford. And so in that moment, when the opportunity came, your imagination came rushing into reality and you became what you had imagined. Once powerful enough, your dreams will demand satisfaction at any cost.

The imagination is the soil from which we grow our lives. It is where we begin the process of creating our lives and living them out in real life. When your heart is dead, when there is hollowness in your soul and God is absent, the imaginations of your heart will run riot and take you places that you should not go. It shapes you into a person none of us actually wants to become.

WILD IMAGINATION

God has an interesting conversation with an Old Testament prophet named Jeremiah. Jeremiah is in prison, but not for committing any crime. He's just obeying God. Needless to say, Jeremiah is not living the life of his dreams, and he's a little ticked off at God. Things are not going well.

Now he's sitting in a prison cell. It's kind of hard to imagine a great life when you're sitting in a cell. It would be a stretch to imagine the endless possibilities and tough to move forward with confidence ("Now I have time to really reflect and create the life of my dreams!") while you're stuck in a cell.

Right then God says to Jeremiah, "Call to me and I will answer you and tell you great and unsearchable things that you do not know." Remember, Jeremiah couldn't see his life from our vantage point. We have the benefit of knowing how the story ends. Generations later, we are shaped by Jeremiah's writings and inspired by his life. He is among an elite few whose life and writings are esteemed as sacred text. Do you think if Jeremiah had known all that would happen through his suffering he would have seen it differently? I am certain of it. Even before Jeremiah's life was anything but desirable, he had already declared he could not turn back or be silent. To live out God's calling for his life was his greatest ambition. This was his dream. Even in his darkest night, Jeremiah was dreaming and living wide awake.

In one sentence, God unwraps for us the power and significance of prayer: "Call to me and I will answer you and tell you great and unsearchable things that you do not know." We think we know what prayer is, but I often wonder. For most of us prayer is when you ask God to solve your problems and tell God what you need and, of course, what you want.

Have you ever considered the possibility that how we pray and how we engage God is pretty much senseless? Do we really think God is saying, "Oh, thanks; I don't know how I missed that. Oh, you need a job? I thought you should be unemployed all your life. Oh, you want a wife? I was going to give you a poodle for Christmas. I'm so glad you're clearing everything up for me"?

When we pray, we act as if God has been missing the point the entire time. "This is what I need, so pay attention, God. Amen." That's not really what prayer is supposed to be about. God invites us to connect on a much more profound level. "Call to me and I will answer you and tell you great and unsearchable things that you do not know."

This is what God is saying: *The reason you need to be in conversation with me is that I created your imagination to be a playground where you and I can get together and I can blow your mind away. I'm going to stretch the boundaries of your dreams. Just ask me, and I will begin to share with you the dreams I have for your life and for all of humanity. You can talk to me about the small stuff, or you can listen to me, and I will let you in on what I am thinking. It's going to be big!*

Remember Adam? He didn't say to God, "God, thanks for the elephants. They're really fun to ride. I'm not so sure about the rhinos; don't ever mount them from the front. God, thanks for everything, but I've got an idea. I need a woman! Koalas are cute, but they're a terrible date." Adam didn't have a clue. He couldn't even conceptualize a woman. God put him in a deep sleep. Why? Because God saw that it was not good for man to be alone. God knew something Adam needed. Something Adam didn't even know he needed. God knew what Adam would want, what Adam would need, something Adam couldn't even imagine.

While Adam was in a deep sleep, God took a rib out of his body and created woman. Then he woke Adam up. When Adam was awakened, he saw Eve and he came alive. He must have given God a standing ovation. God was not only the Creator but also creative. He must have thanked God for not limiting himself to Adam's ability to imagine: "Woman was a great idea! Thanks, God. It never even occurred to me. I didn't know we could be a complementary set. I'll give up a rib for an Eve anytime. Thank you, God."

God knew Adam longed for Eve when Adam himself couldn't even imagine her. Isn't it possible that the life that your soul longs for is beyond even your imagination? Is it possible that no matter how big your dreams are, how expansive your imagination, how ambitious your goals, they pale in comparison to what you would begin to see for your life if you would invite God into your life conversation? He is saying to you, "Call to me and I will answer you and tell you great and unsearchable things that you do not know."

DREAMERS AND VISIONARIES

Joel and Peter are visionaries in the Bible who press us to understand that this is precisely why Jesus came into the world. Joel was an Old Testament prophet who gave us a picture of what would happen to humanity when the Messiah would come. He foreshadows what the movement of Jesus would look like: when God steps into human history and takes on flesh and blood and walks among us, he says, something extraordinary is going to happen to humanity.

And afterward, I will pour out my Spirit on all people. Your sons and daughters will prophesy, your old men will dream dreams, your young men will see visions. Even on my servants, both men and women, I will pour out my Spirit in those days.

Of course a few verses later, Joel writes the verse that is well known by so many people. "Everyone who calls on the name of the LORD will be saved." We tend to translate this to mean that we will be saved in eternity, but that is not what he is focusing on here. You see, God created you in his image and likeness. He created you to be the flesh-and-blood reality of God-sized dreams.

What Joel is saying is that the evidence that Jesus is the Christ, the Messiah, the Son of God, that Jesus is what our souls long for is nothing less than this: God himself will come and dwell within us, and his Spirit will live in us and energize in us dreams and visions beyond our wildest imagination.

The movement of Jesus is a movement of dreamers and visionaries. The proof that Jesus is God is that his followers become a new kind of humanity. In a world that is at best asleep, Jesus awakens us to what it means to be fully alive.

In the New Testament, the apostle Peter chose this passage from Joel to introduce people to this new movement after Jesus had been raised from the dead. This is a movement where dreams and visions are going to be unleashed, and men and women and children will not simply exist, they will not simply sleep through their lives, but they will come to life, and the dreams of God will be awakened.

The apostle Paul prays a prayer for the Ephesians that carries this same conviction. We are in the middle of a movement where God invades our imagination and makes our dreams a reality.

For this reason I kneel before the Father, from whom every family in heaven and on earth derives its name. I pray that out of his glorious riches he may strengthen you with power through his Spirit in your inner being, so that Christ may dwell in your hearts through faith. And I pray that you, being rooted and established in love, may have power, together with all the Lord's people, to grasp how wide and long and high and deep is the love of Christ, and to know this love that surpasses knowledge—that you may be filled to the measure of all the fullness of God.

Here it is, the apex of his prayer:

Now to him who is able to do immeasurably more than all we ask or imagine, according to his power that is at work within us.

What Paul is saying is this: we were created to live in communion with God, and if we would open our lives to God, Jesus would come and dwell within the very core of our hearts. His Spirit, his presence, will energize us and bring us to life and awaken our souls. As we come alive, we will begin to swim in the vastness of God's endless love, and we will discover that his love is even greater than our hopes.

He prays that we will discover that God's intention is greater than our imaginations. We will find how long and how wide and how high and how deep is the love of God, and we will begin to live in the fullness of God—and *then* we will begin to discover what it means to live. We would connect to the One who is waiting to do immeasurably more than we could ever ask or imagine by his power living within us.

Your imagination is a gift. When you enter a relationship with the God who created you, you are awakened, you come alive, and all of a sudden you begin to live the life you were born to live. You were created on purpose. You were created with purpose, for a purpose.

Every day across the world, someone who has lost his hopes and dreams begins to dream again. Someone who has lost her childlike capacity to imagine a better world begins to dream with her eyes open. Someone who has lost hope that he could have a life greater than the one he has is awakened by God and comes alive.

Imagine Being Human

Jesus says:

> I know your deeds; you have a reputation of being alive, but you are dead. Wake up! Strengthen what remains and is about to die, for I have found your deeds unfinished in the sight of my God. Remember, therefore, what you have received and heard; hold it fast, and repent. But if you do not wake up, I will come like a thief, and you will not know at what time I will come to you."

Do you have a reputation of being alive? One of the best compliments I ever received was when a person I had just met said, "Life just pours out of you." I treasure that description. It gives me something to aspire for and live up to. God sees right through us and knows when we are dead. He says, "Wake up! Strengthen what remains. Reclaim your life. Strengthen what remains and is about to die." You can feel when your soul is dying and you are drowning in the mundane. You can barely make it through the day. You never really live—you just exist.

"For I have found your deeds unfinished in the sight of my God" (v. 2 TNIV). You are a masterpiece waiting to be finished. No matter where you've been or what you've done or how badly you've messed up your life, no matter how deeply you've been hurt or have hurt others, you are still a masterpiece in waiting. What a tragedy to breathe your last breath and to discover that your life was not only unfinished, but also perhaps never really even began.

"Remember, therefore, what you have received and heard; hold it fast, and repent" (v. 3 TNIV). To *repent* is to change your mind—to see things in a new way. Whenever we begin to see things from the eyes of God, we must reframe our view of reality.

"But if you do not wake up, I will come like a thief, and you will not know at what time I will come to you" (v. 3 TNIV). Sometimes the Scriptures describe us as asleep and call us to awaken. At other times they tell us we are dead and need to be brought to life. In either case, what we can know is this: God sees what our lives could be in him and what they are without him. When we get even the smallest glimpse of what he sees, we begin to dream of the life we could have, the life we should have.

Don't just dream about living; have the courage to live the life of your dreams. It can begin right here and right now. It begins when you realize that you've been asleep, you've been the walking dead. It's time to wake up! Come alive, be awakened, invite the living God to step into your life, invite Christ to dwell within your soul, to bring you to life. Two thousand years ago, Jesus died a brutal death on an infamous cross on your behalf and mine. All so that we might live—truly, genuinely, and beautifully live.

Maybe you have been asleep. You have never lived up to your potential. You have unfulfilled dreams and longings. If you're dead, let Jesus raise you up to new life. If you have been sleep walking, it's time to wake up and start dreaming wide awake. If you're a sleeper waiting for your wake-up call, then hear his voice to you, "Arise, shine; for your light has come, and the glory of the LORD has risen upon you."

May you never again wake with that little bit of sadness in the mornings. May your every breath be a source of inspiration. You always knew you were created for more; now you can live it out. Go. Dream big. Dream God-sized dreams and have the courage to live them. If you do, the world will never be the same again.

Never again surrender to the thought, *Well, I'm only human.* There is no "only" before human. You are human—created in the image of God. No matter how bad things seem, never forget who you and where you came from. It is a gift to be human. Human— what Jesus became when he took on flesh and blood. Human— what angels can never become. Human—spirit wrapped up in skin. Humanity—the ones for whom Jesus died. That's us, you and me.

Through Jesus' death and resurrection, he came to awaken humanity. To bring us back to life. To us he entrusted creation. To us he entrusted his kingdom. To us he entrusted the future. Can you even begin to imagine the possibilities?

Tomorrow will soon be upon us, and we have much work to do. Time waits for no one. So when the morning comes, after you've hit the alarm and transition from sleep to consciousness, don't forget to live and to dream wide awake.

scripture verses index

Free—10 Music Downloads! And Register to Win an iPod Touch!

To enter this contest, submit a 200 word essay in writing or a 2 minute video telling/showing how you are living your life "wide awake," as exhibited in the book. To submit your contest entry, go to www.erwinmcmanus.com/wideawake and follow the instructions. The first 2,000 entrants will receive 10 free music downloads of their choice. Upon submitting an entry, entrants must provide a valid mailing address in order to receive the free music download cards. All entries must be received by 11:59 p.m. CST December 1, 2008 ("Deadline") to be eligible. Limit one (1) entry per person and per e-mail address. More details at

www.erwinmcmanus.com/wideawake